Modern Critical Interpretations

William Faulkner's
Light in August

Modern Critical Interpretations

The Oresteia
Beowulf
The General Prologue to
  The Canterbury Tales
The Pardoner's Tale
The Knight's Tale
The Divine Comedy
Exodus
Genesis
The Gospels
The Iliad
The Book of Job
Volpone
Doctor Faustus
The Revelation of St.
  John the Divine
The Song of Songs
Oedipus Rex
The Aeneid
The Duchess of Malfi
Antony and Cleopatra
As You Like It
Coriolanus
Hamlet
Henry IV, Part I
Henry IV, Part II
Henry V
Julius Caesar
King Lear
Macbeth
Measure for Measure
The Merchant of Venice
A Midsummer Night's
  Dream
Much Ado About
  Nothing
Othello
Richard II
Richard III
The Sonnets
Taming of the Shrew
The Tempest
Twelfth Night
The Winter's Tale
Emma
Mansfield Park
Pride and Prejudice
The Life of Samuel
  Johnson
Moll Flanders
Robinson Crusoe
Tom Jones
The Beggar's Opera
Gray's Elegy
Paradise Lost
The Rape of the Lock
Tristram Shandy
Gulliver's Travels

Evelina
The Marriage of Heaven
  and Hell
Songs of Innocence and
  Experience
Jane Eyre
Wuthering Heights
Don Juan
The Rime of the Ancient
  Mariner
Bleak House
David Copperfield
Hard Times
A Tale of Two Cities
Middlemarch
The Mill on the Floss
Jude the Obscure
The Mayor of
  Casterbridge
The Return of the Native
Tess of the D'Urbervilles
The Odes of Keats
Frankenstein
Vanity Fair
Barchester Towers
The Prelude
The Red Badge of
  Courage
The Scarlet Letter
The Ambassadors
Daisy Miller, The Turn
  of the Screw, and
  Other Tales
The Portrait of a Lady
Billy Budd, Benito Cer-
  eno, Bartleby the Scriv-
  ener, and Other Tales
Moby-Dick
The Tales of Poe
Walden
Adventures of
  Huckleberry Finn
The Life of Frederick
  Douglass
Heart of Darkness
Lord Jim
Nostromo
A Passage to India
Dubliners
A Portrait of the Artist as
  a Young Man
Ulysses
Kim
The Rainbow
Sons and Lovers
Women in Love
1984
Major Barbara

Man and Superman
Pygmalion
St. Joan
The Playboy of the
  Western World
The Importance of Being
  Earnest
Mrs. Dalloway
To the Lighthouse
My Antonia
An American Tragedy
Murder in the Cathedral
The Waste Land
Absalom, Absalom!
Light in August
Sanctuary
The Sound and the Fury
The Great Gatsby
A Farewell to Arms
The Sun Also Rises
Arrowsmith
Lolita
The Iceman Cometh
Long Day's Journey Into
  Night
The Grapes of Wrath
Miss Lonelyhearts
The Glass Menagerie
A Streetcar Named
  Desire
Their Eyes Were
  Watching God
Native Son
Waiting for Godot
Herzog
All My Sons
Death of a Salesman
Gravity's Rainbow
All the King's Men
The Left Hand of
  Darkness
The Brothers Karamazov
Crime and Punishment
Madame Bovary
The Interpretation of
  Dreams
The Castle
The Metamorphosis
The Trial
Man's Fate
The Magic Mountain
Montaigne's Essays
Remembrance of Things
  Past
The Red and the Black
Anna Karenina
War and Peace

These and other titles in preparation

Modern Critical Interpretations

William Faulkner's
Light in August

Edited and with an introduction by
Harold Bloom
Sterling Professor of the Humanities
Yale University

Chelsea House Publishers ◇ *1988*

NEW YORK ◇ NEW HAVEN ◇ PHILADELPHIA

Printed and bound in the United States of America

10 9 8 7 6 5 4 3 2 1

∞ The paper used in this publication meets the minimum
requirements of the American National Standard for Permanence
of Paper for Printed Library Materials, Z39.48-1984.

Library of Congress Cataloging-in-Publication Data
William Faulkner's Light in August.
   (Modern critical interpretations)
   Bibliography: p.
   Includes index.
   1. Faulkner, William, 1897-1962. Light in August.
I. Bloom, Harold.   II. Series.
PS3511.A86L579   1988   813'.52   87-27655
ISBN 1-55546-047-X

Contents

Editor's Note

This book brings together a representative selection of the best critical interpretations of William Faulkner's novel *Light in August*. The critical essays are reprinted here in the chronological order of their original publication. I am grateful to Johann Pillai and Paul H. Barickman for their erudite aid in my editing of this volume.

My introduction centers upon the stately and loving figure of Lena Grove, the pastoral representation of what is positive in Faulkner's greatest novel, which I contextualize in its author's troubled sense of the genealogy of his own imagination.

Donald M. Kartiganer begins the chronological sequence of criticism with a discussion of Joe Christmas, who as a mulatto is "the Faulknerian symbol of what is beyond comprehension or art." In a Lacanian reading that purports to be Freudian, André Bleikasten describes how the novel's outcasts—Joe, Joanna, even Hightower—relate to absent fathers and patrilineal culture.

Carolyn Porter concentrates on Hightower, whose detached and contemplative stance is defeated because he cannot redeem the past by dwelling upon the dead. Joe Christmas moves back to the center of concern in Eric J. Sundquist's analysis of how Joe embodies the duality of the color line that divides our nation.

James A. Snead argues that because Joe refuses "signification," both the residents of Jefferson and Faulkner's readers tend to combine in fixing the identity of "nigger" upon him. In this volume's final essay, John N. Duvall studies the variations in Joe's relationships with women, and meditates upon why the town of Jefferson calls Joe's crime a "murder" rather than a "killing."

Introduction

No critic need invent William Faulkner's obsessions with what Nietzsche might have called the genealogy of the imagination. Recent critics of Faulkner, including David Minter, John T. Irwin, David M. Wyatt, and Richard H. King, have emphasized the novelist's profound need to believe himself to have been his own father in order to escape not only the Freudian family romance and literary anxieties of influence, but also the cultural dilemmas of what King terms "the Southern family romance." From *The Sound and the Fury* through the debacle of *A Fable*, Faulkner centers upon the sorrows of fathers and sons, to the disadvantage of mothers and daughters. No feminist critic ever will be happy with Faulkner. His brooding conviction that female sexuality is closely allied with death seems essential to all of his strongest fictions. It may even be that Faulkner's rhetorical economy, his wounded need to get his cosmos into a single sentence, is related to his fear that origin and end might prove to be one. Nietzsche prophetically had warned that origin and end were separate entities, and for the sake of life had to be kept apart, but Faulkner (strangely like Freud) seems to have known that the only Western trope participating neither in origin nor end is the image of the father.

By universal consent of critics and common readers, Faulkner now is recognized as the strongest American novelist of this century, clearly surpassing Hemingway and Fitzgerald, and standing as an equal in the sequence that includes Hawthorne, Melville, Mark Twain, and Henry James. Some critics might add Dreiser to this group; Faulkner himself curiously would have insisted upon Thomas Wolfe, a generous though dubious judgment. The American precursor for Faulkner was Sherwood Anderson, but perhaps only as an impetus; the true American forerunner is the poetry of T. S. Eliot, as Judith L. Sensibar demonstrates. But the truer precursor for Faulkner's fiction is Conrad, inescapable for the American novelists of Faulkner's generation, including Hemingway and Fitzgerald. Comparison to Conrad is dangerous for any novelist, and clearly Faulkner did not achieve a *Nostromo.* But his work of the decade 1929–39 does include four permanent books: *The Sound and the Fury, As I Lay Dying, Light in August,* and *Absalom, Absalom!* If one adds *Sanctuary* and *The Wild Palms,* and *The Hamlet* and *Go Down, Moses* in the early forties, then the combined effect is extraordinary.

From Malcolm Cowley on, critics have explained this effect as the consequence of the force of mythmaking, at once personal and local. Cleanth Brooks, the rugged final champion of the New Criticism, essentially reads Faulkner as he does Eliot's *The Waste Land,* finding the hidden God of the normative Christian tradition to be the basis for Faulkner's attitude towards nature. Since Brooks calls Faulkner's stance Wordsworthian, and finds Wordsworthian nature a Christian vision also, the judgment involved necessarily has its problematical elements. Walter Pater, a critic in a very different tradition, portrayed a very different Wordsworth in terms that seem to me not inapplicable to Faulkner:

> Religious sentiment, consecrating the affections and natural regrets of the human heart, above all, that pitiful awe and care for the perishing human clay, of which relic-worship is but the corruption, has always had much to do with localities, with the thoughts which attach themselves to actual scenes and places. Now what is true of it everywhere, is truest of it in those secluded valleys where one generation after another maintains the same abiding place; and it was on this side, that Wordsworth apprehended religion most strongly. Consisting, as it did so much, in the recognition of local sanctities, in the habit of connecting the stones and trees of a particular spot of earth with the great events of life, till the low walls, the green mounds, the half-obliterated epitaphs seemed full of voices, and a sort of natural oracles, the very religion of those people of the dales, appeared but as another link between them and the earth, and was literally a religion of nature.

A kind of stoic natural religion pervades this description, something close to the implicit faith of old Isaac McCaslin in *Go Down,*

Moses. It seems unhelpful to speak of "residual Christianity" in Faulkner, as Cleanth Brooks does. Hemingway and Fitzgerald, in their nostalgias, perhaps were closer to a Christian ethos than Faulkner was in his great phase. Against current critical judgment, I prefer *As I Lay Dying* and *Light in August* to *The Sound and the Fury* and *Absalom, Absalom!*, partly because the first two are more primordial in their vision, closer to the stoic intensities of their author's kind of natural piety. There is an *otherness* in Lena Grove and the Bundrens that would have moved Wordsworth, that is, the Wordsworth of *The Tale of Margaret, Michael,* and *The Old Cumberland Beggar.* A curious movement that is also a stasis becomes Faulkner's pervasive trope for Lena. Though he invokes the imagery of Keats's urn, Faulkner seems to have had the harvest-girl of Keats's *To Autumn* more in mind, or even the stately figures of the *Ode to Indolence.* We remember Lena Grove as stately, calm, a person yet a process, a serene and patient consciousness, full of wonder, too much a unitary being to need even her author's variety of stoic courage.

The uncanniness of this representation is exceeded by the Bundrens, whose plangency testifies to Faulkner's finest rhetorical achievement. *As I Lay Dying* may be the most original novel ever written by an American. Obviously it is not free of the deepest influence Faulkner knew as a novelist. The language is never Conradian, and yet the sense of the reality principle is. But there is nothing in Conrad like Darl Bundren, not even in *The Secret Agent. As I Lay Dying* is Faulkner's strongest protest against the facticity of literary convention, against the force of the familial past, which tropes itself in fiction as the repetitive form of narrative imitating prior narrative. The book is a sustained nightmare, insofar as it is Darl's book, which is to say, Faulkner's book, or the book of his daemon.

II

Canonization is a process of enshrining creative misinterpretations, and no one need lament this. Still, one element that ensues from this process all too frequently is the not very creative misinterpretation in which the idiosyncratic is distorted into the normative. Churchwardenly critics who assimilate the Faulkner of the thirties to spiritual, social, and moral orthodoxy can and do assert Faulkner himself as their preceptor. But this is the Faulkner of the fifties, Nobel laureate, State Department envoy and author of *A Fable,* a book of a badness simply astonishing for Faulkner. The best of the normative critics, Cleanth Brooks, reads even *As I Lay Dying* as a quest for community, an exaltation of the family, an affirmation of Christian values. The Bundrens manifestly constitute one of the most terrifying visions of the family romance in the history of literature. But their extremism is not eccentric in the 1929–39 world of Faulkner's fiction. That world is founded upon a horror of families, a limbo of outcasts, an evasion of all values other than stoic endurance. It is a world in which what is silent in the other Bundrens speaks in Darl, what is veiled in the Compsons is uncovered in Quentin. So tangled are these returns of the repressed with what continues to be estranged that phrases like "the violation of the natural" and "the denial of the human" become quite meaningless when applied to Faulkner's greater fictions. In that world, the natural is itself a violation and the human already a denial. Is the weird quest of the Bundrens a violation of the natural, or is it what Blake would have called a terrible triumph for the selfish virtues of the natural heart? Darl judges it to be the latter, but Darl luminously denies the sufficiency of the human, at the cost of what seems schizophrenia.

Marxist criticism of imaginative literature, if it had not regressed abominably in our country so that now it is a travesty of the dialectical suppleness of Adorno and Benjamin, would find a proper subject in the difficult relationship between the 1929 business panic and *As I Lay Dying*. Perhaps the self-destruction of our delusive political economy helped free Faulkner from whatever inhibitions, communal and personal, had kept him earlier from a saga like that of the Bundrens. Only an authentic seer can give permanent form to a prophecy like *As I Lay Dying,* which puts severely into question every received notion we have of the natural and the human. Darl asserts he has no mother, while taunting his enemy brother, Jewel, with the insistence that Jewel's mother was a horse. Their little brother, Vardaman, says, "My mother is a fish." The mother, dead and undead, is uncannier even than these children when she confesses the truth of her existence, her rejecting vision of her children:

> I could just remember how my father used to say that the reason for living was to get ready to stay dead a long time. And when I would have to look at them day after day, each with his and her single and selfish thought, and blood strange to each other blood and strange to mine, and think that this seemed to be the only way I could get ready to stay dead, I

would hate my father for having ever planted me. I would look forward to the times when they faulted, so I could whip them. When the switch fell I could feel it upon my flesh; when it welted and ridged it was my blood that ran, and I would think with each blow of the switch: Now you are aware of me! Now I am something in your secret and selfish life, who have marked your blood with my own for ever and ever.

This veritable apocalypse of any sense of otherness is no mere "denial of community." Nor are the Bundrens any "mimesis of essential nature." They are a super-mimesis, an over-representation mocking nature while shadowing it. What matters in major Faulkner is that the people have gone back, not to nature but to some abyss before the Creation-Fall. Eliot insisted that Joyce's imagination was eminen·'y orthodox. This can be doubted, but in Faulkner's case there is little sense in baptizing his imagination. One sees why he preferred reading the Old Testament to the New, remarking that the former was stories and the latter, ideas. The remark is inadequate except insofar as it opposes Hebraic to Hellenistic representation of character. There is little that is Homeric about the Bundrens, or Sophoclean about the Compsons. Faulkner's irony is neither classical nor romantic, neither Greek nor German. It does not say one thing while meaning another nor trade in contrasts between expectation and fulfillment. Instead, it juxtaposes incommensurable realities: of self and other, of parent and child, of past and future. When Gide maintained that Faulkner's people lacked souls, he simply failed to observe that Faulkner's ironies were biblical. To which an amendment must be added. In Faulkner, only the ironies are biblical. What Faulkner's people lack is the blessing; they cannot contend for a time without boundaries. Yahweh will make no covenant with them. Their agon therefore is neither the Greek one for the foremost place nor the Hebrew one for the blessing, which honors the father and the mother. Their agon is the hopeless one of waiting for their doom to lift.

III

There are exceptions to the ironic laws of tragic farce even in Faulkner, by which I mean major Faulkner, 1928–1942. The Faulkner of the later forties and the fifties, author of *A Fable* and other inadequate narratives, had been abandoned by the vision of the abyss that had given him *As I Lay Dying* and *Sanctuary*. But even in his fourteen years of nihilistic splendor, he had invented a few beings whose mythic sense of persistence conveys a sense of the biblical blessing. I have already remarked on Lena Grove's stately role as a version of the harvest-girl in Keats's *To Autumn*. Rather than discuss Joe Christmas or Joanna Burden or Hightower, I will center only upon Lena, a vision Wordsworthian and Keatsian, and more satisfying as such than anything akin to her since George Eliot and Thomas Hardy.

One way of seeing the particular strength of *Light in August* as against Faulkner's other major novels is to speculate as to which could contain Lena. Her massively persuasive innocence hardly could be introduced into *The Sound and the Fury* or *Absalom, Absalom!,* and would destroy utterly *As I Lay Dying* or *Sanctuary*. Natural sublimity, Wordsworthian and almost Tolstoyan, requires a large cosmos if it is to be sustained. *As I Lay Dying* is Faulkner's most original fiction and my own favorite among all modern American narratives, yet *Light in August* must be Faulkner's grandest achievement. The book's ability to hold Lena as well as Joe, Joanna, and Hightower, makes it the American novel of this century, fit heir of Melville, Hawthorne, Mark Twain. Difficult as it is to imagine Henry James getting through *Light in August* (after all, he had trouble with Dickens!), the book might have shown James again some possibilities that he had excluded.

Albert J. Guerard, perhaps too absorbed in tracing Faulkner's indubitable misogyny, assimilated Lena to "the softer menace of the fecund and the bovine," but offered as evidence only that "she is, at her best, a serenely comic creation." Fecund certainly, bovine certainly not, and to "serenely" add the further modifier "loving." Judith Bryant Wittenberg, in her feminist consideration of Faulkner, startles me by linking Lena Grove to Joe Christmas, because they "are both products of an exploited childhood now restlessly on the move and aggressive in different ways." Rather, Lena is never-resting, Joe is restless; Joe is aggressive, but Lena moves on, a natural force, innocent and direct but free of the death drive, which is incarnated in Joe, Joanna, and so many others in the novel.

John T. Irwin, keen seer of repetition and revenge in Faulkner, intimates that the association of Lena with Keats's Grecian Urn necessarily links her also to Faulkner's consciousness of his own mortality and to his acceptance of his own writing as a form of dying. Nevertheless, Lena is certainly one of the most benign visions of a reality principle imaginable, and I return to my own Paterian conviction that she resembles the creations of Pater's Wordsworth more than the figures of Keats's tragic naturalism. Lena may be a projection of comic pastoral, but she seems to me more pastoral than comic, and an image of natural goodness invested by Faulkner's genius with considerable aesthetic dignity.

What would *Light in August* be like without her? The story of Joe Christmas and Joanna is almost unrelievedly bitter, though redeemed by its extraordinary social poignance. Hightower is a superb representation of Southern Romanticism destroying itself, while generating a great music from the destruction. What was strongest and clearest in Faulkner's narrative imagination prompted him to place Lena, who gives us a sense of time without boundaries, at the visionary center of the novel. She hardly unifies the book, but *Light in August* has an exuberant abundance that can dispense with an overt unity. Lena will be "light in August," when her child is born, but she is most of the light that the novel possesses throughout. Perhaps she is the answer, in Faulkner, to the poet's old prayer: "make my dark poem light."

The Meaning of Form
in *Light in August*

Donald M. Kartiganer

Light in August is the strangest, the most difficult of Faulkner's novels, a succession of isolated, brilliantly etched characters and scenes that revolve around, finally blur into, an impenetrable center—the character Christmas. As remote from us and his author as he is from the society around him, Christmas withholds some ultimate knowledge of himself, some glimpse into the recesses of being which we feel necessary to understanding. Yet just as obvious as his distance is the fact that he epitomizes every character and movement in the book. Whatever is in *Light in August* is here archetypally in this figure whose very name begins his mystery: Joe Christmas. He is, as Alfred Kazin has observed, "compelling rather than believable," a character who "remains as he is born, an abstraction" (in Hoffman and Vickery, eds.). Like an art image that has never had the privilege of being human, he is never to be merely "believed"; yet at the last he is to "rise soaring into their memories forever and ever. They are not to lose it."

The mystery of Christmas, which doubtless for Faulkner begins, prior to the novel's turning it to account, with the opacity of the mulatto and an uneasiness concerning miscegenation, would appear at first to be the weakness of the novel. Yet this mystery is the meaning of *Light in August,* for the impenetrability of Christmas becomes the only way Faulkner can articulate a truly inhuman, or larger-than-human, wholeness of being of which the others—Lena, Hightower,

From *The Fragile Thread: The Meaning of Form in Faulkner's Novels.* © 1979 by the University of Massachusetts Press.

Byron, Joanna, Hines, Grimm—are the human shadows. For us, they are the recognizable figures for which we read novels; they explain Christmas in their freedom from his special agony of seeming not quite born. In reality it is he who explains them, these "characters" who solidify into crisp, static shapes only because they are less than he. Dimly aware of the pursuit of self that ensures Christmas's isolation, they assume the roles that guarantee their place at least on the edge of society, and to those roles, as well, of the comprehensible figures of fiction. They are not only the visible, partial reflections of the wholeness which is Christmas's suffering, but what Faulkner himself returns to at last: the people he must portray as the bright fragments of the mystery in his book that is necessarily beyond him.

Although *Light in August* is not told as a series of voices, its structure retains the fragmentariness of Faulkner's earlier novels. Through a narrative that juxtaposes blocks of seemingly unrelated material, *Light in August* creates a quality of incoherent mosaic. Despite the fragmentation, however, *Light in August* moves toward a resolution of the problems of *The Sound and the Fury* and *As I Lay Dying*: the broken form, the incompatibility of twin commitments to flux and design, process and product. *Light in August* is dominated by the imagery of dualism: whiteness and blackness; hardness and softness; the "cold hard air of white people" and "the fecundmellow voices of negro women"; "the far bright rampart of the town" and "the black pit . . . the original quarry, abyss itself": all the patterns in which people confine their lives and the violence that threatens and finally breaks loose. This dualism, however, transforms itself into a dynamic in the figure of Joe Christmas.

At the center of *Light in August* is the mulatto—more important, the *imagined* mulatto. This is the role that Christmas, never being sure of what his origins are, has chosen. Able to "pass," to choose a single identity, Christmas chooses instead his doubleness. The only identity that will satisfy him is the one which, in Faulkner's South, is no identity at all, but rather an image of disorder. As a black worker at the orphanage to which Christmas is sent as a child says to him: " 'You dont know what you are. And more than that, you wont never know. You'll live and you'll die and you wont never know.' "

Missing from Christmas is the kind of stable and consistent meaning that fictional characterization and the context of the novel insist on: a stability based, as we shall see, on repression and commitment to a fixed pattern. Being neither black nor white, Christmas is doomed to indefiniteness. And yet he is more than blankness. On the one hand he *is* a life, a structure, a single character—difficult yet visible, lacking the clarity of Hightower and Lena and Joanna, yet capable of being summoned up in our minds by the words "Joe Christmas." On the other hand, he is the disorder that lives always at or near the surface of *Light in August,* the chaos of mixed bloods that brings forth from the life of Jefferson an inevitable violence. The mulatto is the Faulknerian symbol of what is beyond comprehension or art; Joe Christmas is the expansion of that symbol into a precarious yet memorable design that both confronts, and is made of, its own disorder.

In other words, Faulkner begins to move toward a more complex idea of fictional meaning, of a way in which a human life and a fictional creation can unveil a vacancy that yet projects a signifying form, a form that is more than a vacancy. The fragmentariness of *The Sound and the Fury* is echoed in the uneven development of *Light in August*—the juxtaposed but incongruous incidents, the major characters (Lena and Joe) who never meet—but these fragments now begin to cohere in tragic dialogue, a modern form in which design emerges as the voice of a chaos that is signified by and subverts that design.

This modern form is epitomized for us in the figure of Christmas, in the process of his fictional existence. His possible black-white division suggests a reality of perpetual making: a reality of forces whose individual identity is problematic and whose projected meeting is an outrage. The stable dialectic of the rest of the novel encounters in Christmas a dynamic that it finds intolerable. The society of Jefferson and the novel *Light in August* are equally threatened by the meaning of Christmas, for the mode of his being and his characterization are equally destructive to society and to fiction. This opposition of town and text to their own center is an irony underlying the whole novel, for Christmas as a character is as inaccessible to the community of Jefferson as he is to *Light in August,* even as he generates the most profound meanings of both. "This face alone," Hightower thinks, "is not clear." He represents an interaction of forces that the novel and Jefferson can only compartmentalize. Black and white, and all they imply, are distinct sectors, carved in stone, except in the example of Christmas.

The book is about this difference between itself and Christmas, its failure to be equal to his story, to live its life in the same struggle between oppositions as he lives his. Failing to portray Christmas according to traditional criteria of characterization, Faulkner yet suggests to us the struggle of which Christmas is made, and thus makes clear the inadequacy of the portrayal. We are given the general shape of Christmas's contradictory actions, but we are never provided full insight into his inner drama.

Faulkner compels his novel to revolve around a shadowy figure, in whom a strange union of forces represents the impossibility of his existence in verbal form. Yet the *fact* of that impossibility is alive in the novel as a palpable guilt: the awareness of a failure to grasp no more surely than society the truth of the man who becomes its victim; the failure to recognize who Joe Christmas really is.

This may sound more complex than it is, for in certain ways we are on familiar modern ground: the articulation in language of the difficulties of language, in this case the creation of a fictional being, the failure of whose portrayal is something like a strategy. The novelist implies the further range of meaning that both undermines the creation yet compounds the significance.

F. R. Leavis, dealing with Conrad's *Heart of Darkness* (an author and work similar to the Faulkner I am trying to describe) and its attempt to suggest levels of horror beyond articulation, makes what is still a forceful argument against this sort of thing: "He is intent on making a virtue out of not knowing what he means. The vague and unrealizable, he asserts with a strained impressiveness, is the profoundly and tremendously significant" (*The Great Tradition*). The answer to such an argument can only be that an art form (the opposite of incoherence) can describe the struggle toward, and even the qualified failure of, art forms. In *Light in August* the failure of the writer to give his central figure a complete fictional life is mirrored by a situation in which society fails to include this figure in its own structure, yet is deeply marked by his life and death. The man who can have no part in the community, who is in fact cast out of it, finally has a most important part. So too, the figure who is never "realized" in the novel comes to dominate it, casting over its strikingly peopled surface an unearthly light that alters everything.

II

Christmas then is clearly the key: in one sense insufficiently developed as a character, he supplies the rest of the novel with significance. For most readers he is a victim who never frees himself from the circle of his crossed blood (real or imagined), and who is killed by a society enraged at his flaunting of the mixture. But Christmas is more than this, more than his victimization. The conflict driving him toward a violent death is also the conflict he in part creates. This death and the form it takes are what he chooses: his own version of "It is finished."

Readers have always been aware of the parallels between Christmas and Christ, yet have rarely known what to do with them. The tendency among Faulkner's best critics has been to avoid clear-cut identification between the two; there seems little enough in common between the personality of the Christ of the Gospels and the central figure in *Light in August*. Yet it appears to me that the daring of Faulkner's creation here is that Christmas *is* a Christ in the novel, a figure whose form—the antithesis in which his personality is rooted, the struggle for a wholeness of identity unknown to human beings—repeats the structure of the life of Christ.

Joe believes that he may be part black, part white. Blackness is for him what it is for the South in which he lives: an unpredictability, an abyss where life is perpetual flow; passive, yet faintly hostile, and never quite understood. Whiteness is the essence of design: cold, hard, manlike, as predictable as behavior in the context of Simon McEachern's iron laws of good and evil, or the cool and lonely street that stretches before Christmas.

Light in August is permeated with the idea of division, but Christmas is unique among the characters in that he is the only one who insists on unifying the forces rather than accepting, indeed depending upon, their separation. Not, as in Lena's case, by having sufficient faith to do away with the duality or, as in Joanna's, by living that duality one element at a time. Rather he searches for a wholeness that serves alike the dual sides of himself.

This quest for wholeness is to some extent a *given* one for Joe: as he is the model of the division known to all, he is also the most extreme example of the novel's prevading fatalism. Of all the characters his life seems the most arbitrarily determined, as if he were invented by minds prior to the maturity of his own. Referring to the circumstances surrounding Joe's birth—Milly's affair with a man possibly part Negro, Hines's assumption of the role of witness to God's inevitable vengeance—Olga Vickery writes that "Joe is born into a myth created for him by others" (*The Novels of William Faulkner*).

This myth that precedes Joe into existence involves more than the mad assumptions of Hines that he is part Negro, the anti-Christ, the incarnation of sin and corruption. It is also formed by the dietitian and

McEachern. From the dietitian Joe learns a relationship blending women, sex, unpredictability, and secrecy; for the five-year-old boy she is an image of disorder, completely unfathomable behavior that explains itself only by shouting " 'You nigger bastard!' " From McEachern, however, he learns the example of rigid definition, the opposite of what he has learned from the dietitian. Joe's foster father provides him with a powerful image of predictability, rooted in the belief in a design fashioned by God of the destined elect and the destined damned. This Calvinistic sense of a preordained order results in an absolutist belief that there are distinct roles prepared for each man and in an insistence, as if a duty to the God who has created those roles, to fulfill them.

To the black-white division, created by Hines and complicated by the dietitian, McEachern's Calvinism adds a commitment to self-knowledge and self-fulfillment. This evolves into the need for Joe to complete his given identity, whatever its nature.

It is in the combination of these influences on Joe's development that we can begin to see the strange dilemma that has been prepared for him. On the one hand he has been informed that his nature is divided between what he will eventually realize are the opposite poles of existence: the black and the white, the fearfully free and the coldly, permanently ordered. On the other hand he has learned a commitment to being what he is, and a hatred of what hypocrisy and cant that would allow him the peace of accepting less. Christmas is committed, then, to a design rooted in contradiction, a narrative whose completion is impossible according to the terms of the world into which he has been born. His quest for order is fatally bound to an endless process, the hopeless reconciliation of black and white.

In one sense he is the inheritor of an externally conceived plot, yet we must note the difference between the situation here and that of *As I Lay Dying*. Addie Bundren's imposed funeral journey, despite the Bundrens' private motives, has much more of the structural priority common to narrative than does the identity Christmas receives from his various inventors. It is not Hines or the dietitian but Joe himself who supplies weight to that possible identity, giving it most of whatever strength it comes to possess. The "given" of Joe's blackness, unlike Addie's journey, does not function as an arbitrary pattern to limit consciousness; and the behavior of Christmas is different from the Bundrens' willingness to honor publicly and dismiss privately the given plot. Joe transforms this pattern into something larger than its origins. He at once obeys and enlarges its outlines, making it responsive to his own emerging identity, completing the narrative of the anti-Christ even as he lifts it to its sublime opposite. Plot in this novel is not the "determinate poetic form" controlling character energy but the unfounded fable that Christmas reinvents and transforms through a continuing act of consciousness.

Christmas is comprised of what Nietzsche called the Dionysian and the Apollonian, the will to destruction and the will to order. Nietzsche's understanding of those concepts and his insistence on the dynamic relationship between them captures the dynamic of Christmas's character and the tragic conflict he epitomizes. Christmas is both the Dionysian force and its verbalization by an Apollonian force, that difficult fusion that Nietzsche said was the focus of every Greek tragedy: "the one true Dionysos appears in a multiplicity of characters, in the mask of warrior hero, and enmeshed in the web of individual will. The god ascends the stage in the likeness of a striving and suffering individual. That he can *appear* at all with this clarity and precision is due to . . . Apollo" (*The Birth of Tragedy,* trans. Francis Golffing).

In Faulkner's terms, this hero is the black man in the appearance of a white, the god in the guise of a human being. He is the meeting ground of the elements that form him: a commitment to a stable design that the chaos of content is forced to deny. Joe Christmas well knows, as does Faulkner, that there is no language, no action, no available myth or version of reality, that will allow him to live the entirety of his contradictory being. His life is spent in the quest for such a possibility, but not in the north or south of his universe does there exist a name for his wholeness. If there is a wholeness available to him at all, it can lie only in the process of his life, a life gathering itself from the polarities of white and black, design and motion: visible, if still beyond discourse or reason, only as the crossed sticks of his conflict and crucifixion.

Yet he drives incessantly toward identity, fiercely defying all attempts to define him by reduction to less than his awareness of himself. To say "toward identity," however, is to suggest possibility of a kind that doesn't really exist in the novel. By the time Joe has arrived in Jefferson, he knows there can be no conclusion to his particular quest; for it is not a quest to achieve, to win, to bring back, but a quest simply to *be.* Design as an unchanging order that seals its identity forever, like Hightower's adolescent memory of daring boys in wartime he can review again and again, always the flames of burning stores in Jefferson, always the same sound of the shotgun concluding a romantic tale—there can be no such design for Christmas because he can never accept the conclusion of a tale. The whole meaning of his life is that it has no such conclusion. Christmas must create his black-whiteness in every action, destroying each action in the next, the white of the black man's prison, the black of the white man's desire. He can conclude nowhere, for the wholeness he embodies is superior to language, conception, society, art, to all the articulations of action; he can only be the perpetual process of himself. Each motion is no more than a momentary definition, a fragment, a lie, but each joins the *succession* of motions that is the identity of Christmas. His life is always living, never has it *been lived;* he exists in persistent change, and pattern is nowhere but in the act of his becoming.

If there is ever a time when Christmas believes that the unity he desires is something he can know within the contexts society and people provide, it is during his relationship with the waitress-prostitute Bobbie Allen. Prior to that relationship Joe is convinced not only that black and white are separate, for there is no question yet of reconciliation, but that he can prevent the invasion of certain forms of that blackness into his own life (despite the fact that he is aware of his own possible blood division). Blackness in this case is the menstruation of women which Joe, influenced by the dietitian, easily connects with unpredictability and chaos: the "periodical filth" that fatally mars "the smooth and superior shape" of women. Despite what is told him of menstruation, Joe is still adolescent enough to be able to think, *"All right. It is so, then. But not to me. Not in my life and my love."*

But on the first of his evening meetings with Bobbie, Joe discovers she is having her period and he responds by striking Bobbie and fleeing to the woods, there to find the trees, "hard trunks . . . hardfeeling, hardsmelling," like the hardness of McEachern's ruthless design but now imperfect. The trees are like "suavely shaped urns in moonlight. . . . And not one was perfect. Each one was cracked and from each crack there issued something liquid, deathcolored, and foul." But unlike Hightower, who also worships the possibility of a pure life, "complete and inviolable, like a classic and serene vase," Christmas gives up this particular version of what order and design mean. He becomes involved with Bobbie despite his initial disgust; more than that he reveals his suspicions about his black blood, not as a weapon as in subsequent encounters, but simply as a part of his identity: the blackness he discloses to her even as he has received and accepted hers.

He even dares to accept favors from Bobbie (or what he assumes to be such), the "mercy," associated with the dietitian, which he has come to associate with all women as a part of chaos. Since mercy is a redemption from design, a reprieve from that order of things every fact points toward, Christmas sees it as the enemy of order, creating dependencies difficult to honor because one's expected role has been changed. The meaning of mercy to Christmas corresponds to the meaning of his own blackness; faced with an undeserved favor, Christmas usually resists as doggedly as if he were contesting the triumph of the blackness within himself. In part this is because he associates the *need* for mercy with the degraded condition of the Negro; the food Joanna Burden prepares for him is *"Set out for the nigger. For the nigger."* To accept such mercy becomes then a retreat from his insistence on living the whole of his identity, the whiteness as well as the blackness of his being. It is therefore remarkable that he *is* prepared to accept favors from Bobbie Allen, even as he is prepared to accept the menstruation symbolizing her female imperfection, or to share with her the suspected truth of his blood division. And so when Joe begins to visit Bobbie in her room, "he did not know at first that anyone else had ever done that. Perhaps he believed that some peculiar dispensation had been made in his favor, for his sake."

Joe discovers that Bobbie is a prostitute, but he is still prepared at the last to marry her, as if his notions of black and white could actually coexist, cancel each other out in the love of a man and a woman. It is this belief of Joe's that gives the episode with Bobbie a curiously idyllic quality, as if his commitment to identity were somehow not hopelessly complicated by his inner division, as if he could actually be, on earth, the black-white man who is loved and accepted as such, and who can find in that acceptance the necessary language with which to know and accept himself. Bobbie, however, faced with the embarrassment of McEachern's attack at the dance hall and with the deeper problem of Joe's possible murder of his foster father, must revert to the categorizations of her society: she must free herself of the relationship with Joe and return him to his unacceptable divisions: " 'Bastard! Son of a bitch! Getting me into a jam, that always treated you like you were a white man.' "

The fifteen-year street of Joe's quest for identity begins here, an identity that depends on his refusal to accept all possible versions of it. His life—the one he insists he has chosen—becomes the series of alternating roles that seem to divide him, but that are really the difficult terms of his wholeness.

The actions of Christmas from that time on are extremely complex, never allowing the kind of simplistic definition society requires. Invariably these actions combine white and black aspects, subtly bringing together opposing characteristics that allow Joe to remain distinct from white and black, even as he includes the wills of each. This is not simply a matter of challenging whites with his blackness, blacks with his whiteness, but with his capacity, his need, for deliberate reversals, to make of contradictory actions a single seam of personality.

Upon his appearance at the sawmill in Jefferson, in the second chapter of the novel, we find him carrying his name like "an augur of what he will do," yet one can interpret it: " 'Is he a foreigner?' 'Did you ever hear of a white man named Christmas?' . . . 'I never heard of nobody a-tall named it.' " Apparently a white man—allowing himself to be thought that anyway—he takes a "negro's job at the mill" as if in subversion of that whiteness. Yet he counters the effect of a menial job with a contemptuous look that is at odds with it. And while no one understands the meaning of these reversals, everyone senses their strangeness.

The climax of his life is the murder of Joanna and his subsequent behavior as he endures his own Passion Week, his every action appearing to contradict the previous one, yet the whole a sequence of man moving in a tortured harmony. The murder is a blend of determinism and deliberateness. Completed in Joe's mind before he performs the act—"*I had to do it. She said so herself*"—it is still an act of self-assertion as well as self-imprisonment. As he remarks earlier, musing over the ease and security of marriage to Joanna: " 'No. If I give in now, I will deny all the thirty years that I have lived to make me what I chose to be.' "

In hiding from his pursuers, in his capture and his subsequent escape, Christmas reveals his commitment to dual forces. In choosing to stay in the area, he demonstrates, according to some, his blackness: " 'show he is a nigger, even if nothing else.' " But though he refuses to leave the county, he has little trouble avoiding his pursuers, and so his believed ignorance becomes his arrogance, the two combining to make clear categorizations of Joe impossible. Putting on the black brogans for which he has traded his city shoes, Christmas "could see himself being hunted by white men at last into the black abyss which had been waiting, trying, for thirty years to drown him and into which now and at last he had actually entered." But as he senses himself moving toward that primal abyss, which is chaos to him—and toward which he has partially moved all his life—he also tries to maintain an *order,* to keep inact an "orderly parade of named and numbered days like fence pickets." Such, of course, is his conception of whiteness, the dry, firm design that closes off a space, marking the boundaries betweeen the understood and the unknown. He inquires about the day of the week, and it becomes evident that in the wildness of his behavior since the murder—fleeing without really trying to escape, pausing to curse God in a Negro church—he is also carrying out the required actions of some ritual in his own mind, completing some design. This design will strike the reader as in some ways similar to the life of Christ (driving the money-changers out of the church, for instance), but its prime importance, it seems to me, is simply the fact of design itself: Christmas is trying to time his capture according to some idea in his own consciousness, according to some pattern that exists prior to the act and that must be fulfilled. Whatever the precise reason—and there is no way of telling what it is—it is important to Christmas that his arrest take place on a certain day, and he chooses the day like a man whose primary concern is not to give himself up on Friday or Wednesday because it is that day, but who is creating an illusion of life *as the fulfillment of an order.* This is a gesture entirely opposed to his sense of an enveloping blackness, the coming chaos where order is annihilated. Yet, even as he moves in the wagon toward Mottstown with his chosen pattern established, the black shoes keep their symbolic import: "the black tide creeping up his legs, moving from his feet upward as death moves."

Joe's capture sustains the dual style which, in his last days especially, becomes so emphatic. His getting a haircut and shave prior to capture, the calm and passivity with which he accepts capture (he doesn't actually give himself up), imply the meekness of a Negro or the contemptuousness of a white man, deliberateness or indifference. The categories of human behavior accepted by the southern community are all evident in Christmas's conduct, yet in such a mixture that Christmas is behaving as neither black nor white: " 'he never acted like either a nigger or a white man. That was it. That was what made the folks so mad.' " He is now the process of both callings, a confluence of forces that violates the foundations of community life and all the individuals in that community.

And he sustains that variation of styles right to the end. Having allowed himself to be captured, without even trying to get out of the county, he seizes the first opportunity to break away from his captors when they reach Jefferson. Supposedly having agreed to accept a life sentence, he then arranges what is likely to mean an immediate execution. Christmas is moving now in a continuous motion of conflicting orders, a motion that Gavin Stevens, commenting on Christmas's last hours, must break into blocks acceptable to the dualistic logic of the community: " 'Because the black blood drove him first to the negro cabin. And then the white blood drove him out of there, as it was the black blood which snatched up the pistol and the white blood which would not let him fire it. And it was the white blood which sent him to the minister.' " Stevens's analysis of Christmas's dilemma depends on the assumption that black and white are irreconcilable: " 'His blood would not be quiet, let him save it. It would not be either one or the other and let his body save itself.' " But the safety and peace Stevens presumes here is the peace Christmas could never accept. This is not his failure but his triumph, not weakness that deprives him of the security of structure, but an inhuman strength that is his rise to a condition above it: design and darkness at one in the supreme fiction of his life.

In the catastrophe of his murder and castration, Joe Christmas becomes the completed paradox of conception and change, the image of what he is and has been:

> Soaring into their memories forever and ever. They are not to lose it, in whatever peaceful valleys, beside whatever placid and reassuring streams of old age, in the mirroring faces of whatever children they will contemplate old disasters and newer hopes. It will be there, musing, quiet, steadfast, not fading and not particularly threatful, but of itself alone serene, of itself alone triumphant.

Like an image of supreme art, a revolving fiction of disparate forces no longer disparate, he is now that which is beyond struggle or the endless arguments with self of which the struggle has been made, beyond dogma and dialectic, crucified into the black-white man—and therefore beyond the separation on which that poor phrase of dualism rests. He will be interpreted in the discourse of those who are in life rather than in art; Gavin Stevens's systematic version of Christmas's oppositions is the first of these interpretations. But Christmas, as he has always been, although not in a language available to him or us, simply is: "of itself alone triumphant."

Joe Christmas is a Christ figure in this novel because he grows into manhood with a conviction both of an unintelligible, unresolvable split within him and a need to live this split into definition, one that is available, as far as he can determine, nowhere on earth. He owes this conviction to the existence of a narrative created independently of him, a mythic structure, fatal, foretelling, in which he believes and on the basis of which he acts, although he is aware that this tale of his origins may be false. The biblical Christ, like Joe, is born into a narrative that precedes him. Also like Joe, his consciousness is not the plaything of a myth, but rather the source of a courage to fulfill what has been foretold, to *be* that atonement of man and God that he believes is the task of his life and death. We may see Christ as merely the completion of a structure created centuries before his existence, the victim not so much of the men who crucify him as he is of the iron narrative that requires his death in order for the world to complete its pattern. But we must see him also as the arbiter of his destiny, not only the God who becomes a man in order to endure the unwinding of a design, but as the man who becomes the God through his willingness to fulfill that design. It is as if in choosing to complete what has been foretold he invests the ancient prophecies, spoken by the lips of men, with meanings larger than they contain.

Christ berates the man who would save him from the disaster ahead: "But how then should the scriptures be fulfilled, that it must be so" (Matthew). And yet he also prays, "My Father, if it be possible, let this cup pass from me; nevertheless, not as I will, but as thou wilt." His words from the cross, "My God, my God, why hast thou forsaken me?" are the triumphant combination of man and God, the outcry of man caught in the chaos of seeing his death without end, and the whisper of God who composes the meaning of that death by quoting a psalm centuries old, transposing chaos into a unifying design. The quotation confirms the oneness of past and present: from the cross it establishes both the validity of prophecy and the identity of the man who speaks: "Jesus was quoting," Thomas Mann has written, "and the quotation meant: 'Yes, it is I!' " (*Essays,* trans. H. T. Lowe-Porter).

Christ's identity as the man-God can be established only by his pursuing the dualism to the end: for him to be rescued from his fate by "twelve legions of angels" would establish only his divinity but not his humanity. On the cross the anguished sufferer and the God who has fulfilled the prophecies are one, suspended in space like a divine image of the experience and meaning of being human. The death confirms the unique wholeness of his life, in which the human and divine, flesh and spirit, have become the inseparable languages of each other.

The basic form of Christ and Christmas is the same; and both come to horrify those communities whose insistent divisions they have chosen to resolve. This element of outrage is, of course, more emphatic in the case of Christmas, whose agony and confusion drive him to murder, whose tale is not told by a believer, as in the Gospels, but by the writer doomed to membership in the community. The violence of introducing a new vision to a world convinced it can do without it is everywhere in the story of Christmas. Faulkner's Christmas, unlike the dull echo of Christ we find in *A Fable,* is a new and striking creation of the *act* of vision, of what it might mean to invent and live a meeting of contradictions: of man and God, of design married to the darkness that destroys and signifies.

III

To move from Christmas to the "characters" of *Light in August* is to move to what is more properly the language of fiction and to fuller, more conventionally realized figures. These characters depend for their identities, in the context both of society and the novel, on the existence of certain patterns: the illusions of order that allow them to live their lives. Each character inherits or creates a pattern that, although it restricts movement and choice, remains a last defense against a reality not to be faced unarmed. These are Apollonian structures built to protect against a chaos too difficult to understand or bear, and thus the characters come to them in gratitude and relief. In Hightower's words, they are the "shapes and sounds with which to guard [themselves] from truth."

Such a use of illusion also characterizes the Jefferson society Faulkner sets up in the novel: a rigid system of white and black, where the black—symbolically the unconscious, the "lightless hot wet primogenitive Female"—is calmed into impotence by being locked within the confines of the city walls. The town has a name for its "reality"—it is called "nigger" and lives in Freedman town—and thus has stabilized it, believing like Hightower (and with considerably more reason) that it has bought its immunity. The black community, in other words, has been drawn into the white-dominated Jefferson community and made subservient to it. If blackness is in this novel a Dionysian or process principle, it has become clearly the servant of an

Apollonian or product order. Blackness is in Jefferson an *image* of chaos and therefore its very opposite, a verbal and social prison for chaos.

All the characters in the novel but Christmas follow the model of Jefferson: they commit themselves to a clear pattern, designed to resist the complexity of actual conditions. One means of carrying out this commitment is the strategy of objectifying an inner reality, transferring fear or desire, a chaos scarcely to be met as one's own, to an object outside the self. The imagination creates illusory patterns that identify and eject those parts of the self too difficult to bear. In several instances Christmas himself becomes the living figure of someone else's inner reality. McEachern and Percy Grimm's identification of Joe as Satan or black rapist is a strategy of psychic survival.

This is not to say that repression is absolute, or illusion invulnerable. On the contrary, it is the frailty of illusion that creates the action of the book. Chaos reveals itself often, sometimes as the temporary anger, a holiday of vengeance, through which community releases its locked up energy; sometimes as that glimpse of the real that even the most dream-ridden, like Hightower, occasionally require. And sometimes we see it as the mad edge of those fanatic orders created by Hines and McEachern: orders which, like all the others, are fed by the fires of chaos, so much so that any relaxation of design must be the outbreak of insanity.

These strategies of survival are the writer's strategies of characterization as well. Their inner chaos objectified, as it can never be for Christmas, McEachern and Grimm gain a certain fixity that allows us to see them. Christmas insists on a total self: he will not know himself, as the others do, in the image of that which he must eventually destroy. His remoteness from us, as opposed to the clarity of McEachern and Grimm, Hightower and Hines, is owing to his unwillingness to accept a split life. Chaos is himself, not a sacrificial object. In creating Christmas, Faulkner challenges an idea of consistency in character for the sake of an idea of change and movement. As Kazin puts it, Faulkner attempts "the tremendous feat of making us believe in a character who in many ways is not a human being at all—but struggling to become one." Character as a struggle toward being becomes Faulkner's subversive act in a novel of otherwise conventional characterization, just as Christmas's insistence on oneness is his own subversive act.

The figure of Hightower is the clearest version in the novel of the human need to encounter reality through protective fantasies. As with Christmas and Joanna Burden, Hightower has inherited the particular forms his need for order will take, his childhood memories of the Civil War experiences of his grandfather and his father. Referring to the horror with which the young Hightower first notices the patch of the Yankee blue on his father's black coat worn during the war, Edmond Volpe observes, "He associates his father with the real world; the story of his grandfather releases him from the terrors of reality." The father's coat, with its array of patches—"Patches of leather, mansewn and crude, patches of Confederate grey weathered leafbrown now" and the patch of blue—is the motley costume of comedy. But the story of the grandfather's raid on Jefferson and his subsequent death in a henhouse is of the single color and clear line of an adolescent's notion of glory:

> "They were boys riding the sheer tremendous tidal wave of desperate living. Boys. Because this. This is beautiful. Listen. Try to see it. Here is that fine shape of eternal youth and virginal desire which makes heroes. . . . It's too fine, too simple, ever to have been invented by white thinking. A negro might have invented it. And if Cinthy did, I still believe. Because even fact cannot stand with it."

Hightower presents the story as a magnificent artifact of color and touch and sound, with the whole circumstance of the war, " 'with all that for background, backdrop: the consternation, the conflagration.' " The death at its close, the disgrace of chicken-stealing, only enhances its beautiful unbelievability for Hightower: " 'It's fine so. Any soldier can be killed by the enemy in the heat of battle, by a weapon approved by the arbiters and rulemakers of warfare. Or by a woman in a bedroom. But not with a shotgun, a fowling piece, in a henhouse.' "

Spurred from the beginning by a tale, Hightower at first attempts to imitate its form by going to seminary, as if in Church he can live in a context where "truth could walk naked and without shame or fear," where life could be "intact and on all sides complete and inviolable, like a classic and serene vase." His aim is to convert his life into the purity of the tale. But the seminary has to give way to a parish, then to the need for a wife; at last he comes to Jefferson, where, as it turns out, he has been headed all the while.

But Hightower's devotion to his bright dream is a process well-told by several of Faulkner's critics. What I would like to concentrate on here is the division of Hightower between his need for design and his still existing need to live, however superficially, in a real world. " 'I am not in life anymore,' " Hightower muses, but his peculiar pathos is that he is, that he is suspended between dream and reality, completely absorbed in neither; and unlike Christmas, he cannot perform the difficult art of bringing them together.

Hightower's sole link to a world outside himself is Byron Bunch, but through Byron he becomes gradually involved with Lena Grove, with the grandparents of Joe Christmas, and finally with Christmas. Reality, it appears, is not easily put aside, and Hightower's delivery of Lena's baby is the culmination of his grudging surrender to its temptation. It is as if he has been goaded back into life, tempted to think it can prove less violent, more manageable than before.

In his return, however, he still must heighten his real action into illusion, his engagement with the real never to be free of the imagination's embellishments: "And then he says it, thinks it. *That child that I delivered. I have no namesake. But I have known them before this to be named by a grateful mother for the doctor who officiated.*" He can even think that " 'luck and life [have] returned to these barren and ruined acres,' " and that he, Gail Hightower, the outcast, the scorned, has been a part of that returning.

These particular extensions of the real are more wedded to action than Hightower's memory of his grandfather's war exploits. Yet in the midst of his new sense of having put aside his ghosts for the flesh of reality, his new pride in falling asleep over *Henry IV* instead of Tennyson, Hightower still gloats over the fact that Byron has abandoned his courtship of Lena and left town. In this respect Hightower is still harboring an addiction to purity, in the wake of new life caressing uncomplex things: " 'If you must marry, there are single women, girls, virgins. It's not fair that you should sacrifice yourself to a woman who has chosen once and now wishes to renege that choice. It's not right. It's not just.' "

But the temptation of the real continues its work on Hightower, and he makes his gesture at the end to save Christmas from Percy Grimm by insisting that Christmas was with him the night Joanna Burden was murdered. It is the climax of his self-abasement, for both the homosexuality and the mulatto murderer must be for Jefferson the maddest kinds of violation of its well-guarded order.

Hightower's confession, however, cannot be seen as a full meeting of the real and the abandonment of illusion. For with this admission, Hightower is also insuring the latest community rejection that will drive him back to the safer confines of his dreaming. Exploiting the image of Joe as black rapist and murderer, and adding a hint of homosexuality, Hightower's confession is motivated not only by humanitarian purposes but by hunger for the bitter privileges of his imaginary world.

So we see him at the end of the novel confronting, one by one, the darkest realities of his lifetime, only to conclude, as always, with the persistent dream that puts realities aside. In chapter 20 he confronts everything: his horror at a coat, his hyprocrisy at the seminary, his service to a church that he believes is a barricade "against truth and . . . peace," his misuse of his pulpit—"a charlatan preaching worse than heresy," the masochistic pride in his torment at the hands of the townspeople—"that patient and voluptuous ego of the martyr." Then the most awful reality of all, that he has been the " 'instrument of [his wife's] despair and shame' . . . *I don't want to think this. I must not think this. I dare not think this.*"

At the conclusion of this confession of perverse desire, Hightower has only summoned new energies to serve the illusion that is still paramount. The ugliness of his life and the ensuing guilt support and provide the power for that enduring illusion which is "honor and pride and life" miraculously distilled from impurity: "It is as though they had merely waited until he could find something to pant with, to be reaffirmed in triumph and desire with." Once again the imaginary riders rush by, dividing illusion from the darkness that has strangely inspired it: "the wild bugles and the clashing sabres and the dying thunder of hooves."

Joanna Burden would appear to be a typical instance in the novel of the need to possess a pattern for existence, in her case the inherited conviction that the Negro is the curse of the white man. This is the pattern that envelops her, and like Hightower's it begins to operate while she is still a child. Leaving little room for consciousness, it ensures a recognition of the forces of black and white as a *duality,* and thus weakens from the beginning any power consciousness might have for breaking through to some version of interaction. This polarity is the result of her father's efforts to derive some meaning from the murder of her grandfather and brother: " 'Your grandfather and brother are lying there, murdered not by one white man but by the curse which God put on a whole race before your grandfather or your brother or me or you were even thought of. A race doomed and cursed to be forever and ever a part of the white race's doom and curse for its sins.' "

To contain violence in a pattern that will justify violence, that will convert it from some eruption of human hate and madness into a comprehensible part of a larger scheme—this is the dominant structure not only of Joanna's life but of the novel in general. The nature of violence is altered: the Dionysian is made not only to serve the Apollonian impulse toward design, but in so doing to lose its brief identity as Dionysian.

As a result of the pattern her father describes, Joanna likewise imagines an absolute narrative: " 'But after that I seemed to see them for the first time not as people, but as a thing, a shadow in which I lived, we lived, all white people, all other people.' " The meaning of her life becomes the effort to rise: " ' "But in order to rise, you must raise the shadow with you." ' "

There is an important difference, however, between Joanna and the other inheritors of pattern, and it is this difference that helps explain why Joe Christmas stays with her for three years, and why he releases himself from her only because he has decided to bring his life to its own meaning and conclusion. Upon meeting Joe, Joanna divides her life in half: a being of day and a being of night, the spinster who methodically carries out her destiny by advising and aiding Negro colleges—by helping black people "rise"—and the frustrated middle-aged woman who spends her nights in sexual orgy with a man she believes or hopes is part Negro. By day she raises the Negro of her imagination to her level and at night lowers herself to his, as if trying in fact to *become* what is for her the principal meaning of the word damned: " 'Negro! Negro! Negro!' "

In one role she is "hard, untearful and unselfpitying and almost manlike," in the other, free of the manlike passion for order, an image for Christmas of a "bottomless morass." By day she remains true to the pattern forced on her by her father, adopts the role of a white woman hung on a cross of blackness; by night she undermines the pattern in the only way she knows how: by becoming the cross itself, with Joe as the instrument of her transformation.

Because of this division, she is the only one in the novel who can believe in and accept Joe's own suspected division. She is not indifferent to his black blood, like the white prostitute in Detroit; yet she is still able to draw Joe into the context of her own design. He contains within himself the polarity of her vision of the world, the saved and the damned, and for a time she is willing, as if in partnership with him, to taste both: salvation by day, damnation by night. Joanna's is by no means a "whole" life, since she takes her design and her chaos one at a time; but she is the closest to Joe in the novel.

Finally, however, she belongs with the believers in order; by the "third phase" of her relationship with Joe she has decided that damnation is done, and the time has come to ascend, this time for good. Having accepted him as a divided being for the purposes of her own tour of hell, Joanna must now nail Joe down as Negro, marry him and/or send him to a Negro college, force him to study with a Negro lawyer and to take over from her the task of raising the Negro: he must raise himself as if he were both Christ and cross. At the end, she wants only for him to kneel with her, to allow her to retreat back to her given role of the white savior of Negroes by letting her pray for him and his black soul. For this is the only way she can redeem her period of damnation, convert it from an indulgence in nymphomania into a necessary humiliation of the self which consumes part of the path to salvation. That she has actually enjoyed her sex with Joe she does not even hide from herself: "What was terrible was that she did not want to be saved. . . . 'Don't make me have to pray yet. Dear God, let me be damned a little longer, a little while.' " But finally she *must* pray, and must raise Joe to college graduate and respectable lawyer; must solidify him into the black role that will justify her sexual relationship with him. More important, she must secure herself in her own original role, the circle of her life she too has never been able to break out of. At the end she does not challenge this given pattern at all, but hopes to reassert it with a clarity consistent with her heritage.

She does not reckon, however, on the stubborn integrity of Joe. For if her life has been lived in the design of a white Christ redeeming the black cross to which she is nailed, then Joe's has been lived in the insistence that he has not succumbed to an imposed design of any sort: that he is black *and* white, and that he will know the full nature of this complexity in his quest for identity. Joanna tries to force Joe to that single side of him which is his blackness; his killing her is, in more ways than one, an act of self-defense.

In McEachern, Hines, and Percy Grimm we see examples of the most mindless commitments to pattern in the novel: not pattern as the heroic, adolescent poem Hightower distills from his past, or as the social commitment Joanna Burden has created out of her conviction of the Negro's God-bestowed inferiority, but pattern as an implacable machine in the shape of God, carving a complex reality into the clear names of good and evil. To be sure, Hightower's fable and Joanna's hope to raise the Negro, like all patterns, must have their victims, the instruments of a wife or a mulatto lover (not to mention the inner being) that are necessary to the service of these designs. Yet McEachern, Hines, and Grimm are possessed by their orders to an extreme not found elsewhere in the novel. In the end, however, these frozen products are invaded, if only momentarily, by the Dionysian chaos that pattern has been intended to close off. This invasion is comparable to the uncharacteristic recklessness of Hightower in moving again toward life, or in risking the lie that Christmas was with him the night of the murder, or to Joanna's three years of nighttime debauchery with Christmas. In the lives of Joe's two "fathers" and his murderer, however, it erupts with a unique savagery, for theirs have been the most regimented and locked-in lives, and the ones in which the spectre of madness has always loomed.

Grimm, we are told, "had been for a long time in a swamp, in the dark" and "his life opened definite and clear. . . . uncomplex and inescapable as a barren corridor, completely freed now of ever again having to think or decide." The National Guard becomes his design, its order, honor, and uniform become the language, the "austerely splendid scraps of his dream." Throughout the chase after Christmas, Grimm maintains a perfect calm and composure appropriate to his chosen vocation: "He ran swiftly, yet there was no haste about him, no effort. There was nothing vengeful about him either, no fury, no outrage." But at the close, confronting the nigger-murderer-homosexual-seducer of white men and women, Grimm is no longer the composed guardsman, joyful in the rigidity of duty, but the maddened avenger whose protective shield has been dislodged for a moment by the sight of Christmas, who is at this point not so much his own Dionysian darkness as Percy Grimm's.

For Hines and McEachern, the last encounter with Joe Christmas is a meeting with the Devil himself: Christmas transformed into a crude Satanic incarnation of his creators' madness. McEachern expresses his discovery of Joe in the last of the sins he has predicted for him—sloth, ingratitude, irreverence, blasphemy, lying, and lechery— with only a sigh, "a sound almost luxurious, of satisfaction and victory." In fulfilling completely the terms of folly, Joe confirms

McEachern's place on the side of right, and confirms as well his foster father's polar vision. But McEachern's calm and assurance are only a delusion of mind when he confronts Joe at the dance hall with Bobbie: "Very likely he *seemed to himself* to be standing just and rocklike and with neither haste nor anger. . . . Perhaps they were not even his hands which struck at the face of the youth" (my emphasis). This is McEachern at the edge of lunacy: "it was not that child's face which he was concerned with: it was the face of Satan, which he knew as well."

Hines has also tried to escape an inner violence through the mad fable of his grandson as the Devil's child. As Volpe has pointed out, "His daughter's sexual adventure provides a focus for his tensions, and his violence is transformed into a blend of religious and racial fanaticism." With such a pattern in mind "the once violent Hines can now sit quietly in the orphanage for five years to watch his grandson." Immersed in the illusion of his own godliness, Hines can wait, "watching and waiting for His own good time"; yet at the end, when Joe quietly allows himself to be captured in Mottstown—"the captive was the only calm one"—Hines is no longer an agent of God but madness maddened: "Impotent and raging, with that light, thin foam about his lips. . . . 'Kill the bastard!' he cried. 'Kill him. Kill him.' "

The eruption of chaos into the once secure limits of order is, generally in a much less furious manner of course, a pattern repeated several times in the novel, for *Light in August* is not only about the attempts of people and societies to preserve an Apollonian-like pattern to their lives, to replace chaos with art, but about the necessary reemergence of that chaos. This is one of the several meanings of the novel's enigmatic title; for the light of August is a "savage summer sunlight," a "shameless savageness." Every figure in the novel must live his moment in this August light when an inner savageness, like the fury of a god long quelled, temporarily destroys the existing orders. And the source of this eruption, *in every case,* is Joe Christmas who, like the hero of Greek tragedy, brings to everyone the knowledge that annihilation looms, that the inevitable wreckage of design must disclose the destructive self.

IV

We come, and none too soon, to less strenuous matters: Lena Grove and Byron Bunch; the very names abolish rage and pain. Lena and Byron are the sources of comedy in *Light in August* and of a kind of affirmation, although perhaps this last has been too uncritically emphasized by readers. Their meeting and subsequent relationship is a triumph of human action in the novel: good, gentle people, winning for themselves a deserved happiness amidst the extremity and obsession surrounding them. And yet it is doubtful that this sense of acceptance and even delight, which opens and closes *Light in August,* relieves the novel from its grimmer sense of human fate, or redeems Jefferson, whose citizens are as happy to see the departure of Lena and Byron as they are of Lucas Burch and Christmas.

There is a kind of irrelevance in Lena. The world of *Light in August* is not her world, and her faith and the luck it brings her are as remote from this novel as Dilsey's faith is from the main thrust of *The Sound and the Fury.* That these are good people and frequently even happy people—old Dilsey singing away over the breadboard, Lena in constant delight at the mere passage of miles—does not alter the fact that they are not quite central to most of what goes on in their books or to the notion of reality those books insist on.

The comedy of Lena Grove is a comedy of faith, a conviction of order so firm that it can hardly be said to be a conscious choice. Walking with assurance out of Doane's Mill as if signposts marked "Lucas Burch, 10 mi." will be set alongside the road; pleased with her ladylike behavior at Armstid's breakfast table; fascinated with the variety of countryside, people, reactions to her—Lena beholds a world she cannot imagine as hostile. The comedy of it all is simply our recognition of that faith as being not only irrelevant to reality but superior to it. Lena's belief that " 'a family ought to all be together when a chap comes' " is the assurance that it will be. The distance between this faith and what we know to be the truth of Lucas Burch and his ilk would normally result in pathos. Here it is comedy because we know that although Lena is obviously wrong about the intentions of her lover, she is also right about her own destiny; we know that contradictions will somehow resolve themselves in her favor, regardless of Lucas Burch. There is a part of Lena, Byron says, that " 'knows that [Lucas] is a scoundrel' "; yet she is not to be bothered with rationalizing the difference between this knowledge and her larger faith. Her attitude is much like Byron's: " 'if the Lord don't see fit to let them two parts meet and kind of compare, then I ain't going to do it either.' "

In a novel primarily about the violent collisions between illusion and reality, Faulkner dares to give importance to the woman who recognizes no disparity between them: illusion *becomes* reality in the comic vision of Lena Grove. Her outlook, as pleasantly and resolutely unswerving as Hines's is fanatically and hatefully unswerving, is the least imaginative creation in the novel, for it is simply a social and religious platitude she has adopted whole. Good girls don't have bastard children—" 'I reckon the Lord will see to that' "—and it isn't going to occur to Lena that she deserves less from God than the next good girl.

Lena's place in *Light in August* has been acutely perceived by Irving Howe, who looks beneath the usual platitudes about Lena: "She stands for the outrageous possibility that the assumption by Faulkner and his cultivated readers may be false: —the assumption that suffering finds a justification in the growth of human consciousness. For Lena is and does 'right' with a remarkably small amount of consciousness or suffering, neither of which she apparently needs very much; she is Faulkner's wry tribute to his own fallibility, a tribute both persuasive and not meant completely to persuade." Insofar as consciousness is concerned and the modernists' grasp of life as a struggle toward full awareness, Lena Grove is the character least relevant, for she is herself barely conscious at all.

There is another, by no means contradictory, way of looking at Lena. This is as the representative of that which makes a struggle toward consciousness quite unnecessary: namely, pure faith. In this respect she is the counterpart of Dilsey, whose faith in *The Sound and the Fury* is the source of the most effective vision in the book—not because it is true to the kinds of reality that novel presents, but because it sustains her, where all other visions are inadequate even to their owners. Like Dilsey, Lena knows within the midst of becoming the being that designs the whole. As Dilsey can say " 'I seed de beginnin, en now I sees de endin,' " so Winterbottom can say of Lena, " 'I reckon she knows where she is going. . . . She walks like it.' " It is characters like Lena and Dilsey who, in the midst of Faulkner novels of chaos and a persistent fragmentation, live lives that are like lives remembered, lives with beginnings, middles, and ends. They move from known beginnings to known conclusions, always aware of the full scope of the history they are in the process of completing.

Opposed to the wholeness Lena represents is Christmas, whose own wholeness is not a given, like grace, but a struggle with divisions he is all too aware of. The chaos that Christmas must engage is the chaos that Lena cannot even see. She possesses by faith what Joe can have only through the Faulknerian route, that is to say, through the tragic route of defining an individual history. Joe ends whole because crucified; crucified because he has dared to create his wholeness. Lena is born into a condition that Joe has had to prove. In more ways than one she inherits her "family" at the end because he has lived and died for it.

Behind Lena, dogged, persevering, is Byron Bunch, the most flexible of men and the most resourceful in breaking out of his self-styled patterns and risking the no-man's land of possibility. At the beginning of *Light in August,* Byron has walled himself into a tight structure of weekday work and Sundays in a country church, created out of a simple acknowledgment that "a fellow is more afraid of the trouble he might have than he ever is of the trouble he's already got." Infatuated at his first meeting with Lena, Byron breaks a prime habit—" 'In town on Sunday night. Byron Bunch in town on Sunday' " —thus quietly but emphatically opening himself to a world of contingency and the need to submit all his carefully built codes to the awkward demands of loving Lena Grove.

He invents new illusions to protect himself from those demands, but he discards them when reality beckons. He pretends that the pregnant Lena is a virgin, only to accept at last, with the cry of her baby, *"that she is not a virgin. . . . It aint until now that I ever believed that he is Lucas Burch. That there ever was a Lucas Burch."* Following his request to the sheriff to send Lucas Burch to see Lena, Byron leaves Jefferson, mistakenly assuming that Lena and Lucas will get married. At the sight of Lucas climbing out the back window of Lena's cabin, he dreams of bringing Lucas *back:* " 'And I may not can catch him, because he's got a start of me. And I may not can whip him if I do, because he is bigger than me. But I can try it. I can try to do it.' " After his beating at the hands of Lucas, and after seeing Lucas ride off on a train, Byron is left with the reality that Lena is, at long last, available.

At this point his imagination comes to a halt, for he is either unable or unwilling to create a fantasy about what is to follow. He can see himself at the door of her cabin easily enough: *"Then I will stand there and I will. . . .* But he can get no further than that." Byron has opened himself to the unpredictabilities of reality in a manner dupli-cated by no one else in the novel except Christmas. Most of the other characters have never discarded their protective illusions; Lena, of course, has never had any need to. But in the name of love, Byron submits himself to the road, the road Lena travels with equanimity because her faith is greater than its surprises, but which Byron must endure as an ordinary man.

If Byron were a more impressive figure, his power at least to begin a course of action free of imaginary preconceptions (apart, of course, from the hope that he will eventually make Lena his wife) might have great significance in the novel. As it is, Byron has merely tied himself to Lena's larger vision, whose authenticity we certainly do not question, but whose relevance to Faulkner's world continues to escape us.

And what of Jefferson, locale and backdrop for all these events? Its division of white and black is an echo of the destructive dualities of the leading characters. We shall not reach the deepest meanings of *Light in August,* however, by attacking the community. It is, for the bulk of the novel, a quiet, peaceful place, precisely because it has worked out a modus vivendi of pattern and desire that enables it to endure and to protect its members. Jefferson may be said to represent the most stable possibilities of an existence basically full of contradiction. Not that it has achieved a genuine interaction of forces by any means, but its illusions are less desperate, less fanatic than those of Hines, McEachern, Joanna, or Grimm, and less remote from reality than those of Hightower.

Significantly enough, Jefferson is able to accommodate even its outcasts—the Hightowers, the Joanna Burdens, the Hineses—allowing all of them (with the important exception of Christmas) to remain within the community, even if on the outskirts. And while some, like Hightower, are made to feel its disapproval, most are the beneficiaries of its tolerance and charity. Hines is considerately escorted home by townspeople who find his fanaticism no saner than do we. Byron Bunch, whose deliberate self-isolation renders him merely invisible for part of the novel, and whose courting of the pregnant Lena makes him into "wellnigh a public outrage and affront" for the rest of it, is in no danger from society. And Joanna and Hightower, whose patterns vary the most from Jefferson's codes, are, until the final days of Christmas, allowed the peace and occasionally even the small generosities of the community.

Most of the life of Jefferson is in fact the life of order, of people who believe that "no matter what a man had done with his Sabbath, to come quiet and clean to work on Monday morning was no more than seemly and right to do." And when violence is at last set loose, aroused by the image of the black murderer Christmas, the town soon reverts to the tranquility of "suppertables on that Monday night," the citizens of Jefferson eating and calmly talking about the strange behavior of Christmas, following his arrest. Jefferson is what is possible and plausible in *Light in August;* its vision is not equal to Christmas, but in this respect it follows a deep precedent. In short, Cleanth Brooks is quite right when he emphasizes the condition of Jefferson as "a matrix, the life of a little Southern community, one which, whatever its limitations, faults, and cruelties, is a true community" (Introduction to *Light in August,* 1st printing, 1932). Between the religious visionary, Lena, who frames the novel, and the evolving Man who lives at its center, we have nowhere to stand but in the community of men and women. As Hightower says, "all that any man can hope for is to be permitted to live quietly among his fellows."

This recognition, however, returns us to the tragedy of the novel, for the failure of Jefferson to comprehend Christmas is a crucifixion. And the need for clarity at the expense of truth which that crucifixion exemplifies is a need implicit not only to the structure of community but to the structure of art as well. The great guilt of Jefferson is that it can find no room within it, not even on its periphery, for Joe Christmas. It has no place for him for the simple reason that he is the one figure in the novel whose sense of the necessary relationship between design and energy is different from its own. But this is the guilt, one must add, of the novel *Light in August* and its author, whose failure to bring Christmas fully into the context of the human becomes a moving admission that community's repressive division may find an echo in the nature of fictional language.

V

All of Faulkner's major novels are studies in fragmentation, experiments in the nature and cause of disorder and in the possibility of working through it to some sense of coherence. As I hope I have already established, the making of coherent form in Faulkner is of prime significance, involving the most crucial issues of consciousness and the possibilities of human community.

In *As I Lay Dying,* following the persistent refusal of *The Sound and the Fury* to accept any of its various imaginative modes, Faulkner uses the long funeral journey of the Bundrens as a means of avoiding the distintegration that befalls the Compsons. With the same structural device he also alters the shape of *As I Lay Dying* from a succession of remote, self-interested voices into a coherent action. The irony, of course, is that awareness, so much of what Addie calls "the duty to the alive, to the terrible blood," has been purged from the novel for the sake of its order, even as the rich consciousness of Darl must be purged from the family as the price of the completion of the journey.

In *Light in August,* however, Faulkner uses far subtler means of ordering disjointed materials. Unlike the "voice" novels, this narrative is told from outside, and from this external point of view Faulkner creates an intricate network of mirror images and metaphoric relationships that unify the book. Despite the novel's considerable fragmentariness, its unrelated characters, its juxtaposition of incongruous events, not to mention Faulkner's usual chronological shifting, *Light in August* achieves a high degree of coherence almost entirely through the use of metaphor: an elaborate series of echoes bringing together in the reader's mind, if not in that of the participating characters, the whole sprawling canvas of *Light in August.*

Michael Millgate has observed:

> Any search for underlying patterns in *Light in August* might well begin with a consideration of the extensive series of parallels and substitutions which appear in the course of the novel and which again establish thematic and even narrative links between its different strands. An obvious example is Mrs. Hines' confused identification of Lena's baby with Joe Christmas when he was a child, and her further reference to the baby as being actually Christmas's son. One thinks also of the similarities between the apparently opposed backgrounds of Hightower and Miss Burden, fanatics of the South and of the North; of the parallelism between the tragic encounter of Joe Christmas with Percy Grimm and the primarily comic encounter of Byron Bunch with Lucas Burch, which takes place at the same moment in time; of the reverberations set up in the reader's mind by the incident of Christmas breaking into a Negro church like an impersonation of the devil, recalling as it does both the mad forays into Negro churches made by his grandfather, Doc Hines, and the moment of Satanic glee caught by the camera as Hightower leaves his empty church.

Most important of all, however, is the relationship be-

tween Miss Burden and Lena Grove and Lena's replacement
of Miss Burden at the plantation after the latter's death.

(*The Achievement of William Faulkner*)

These links are indisputable; and one can go even further in itemizing
them since they exist, usually in less striking manner, all through the
novel.

Lena's four-week journey from Doane's Mill to Jefferson, for example, "is a peaceful corridor paved with unflagging and tranquil
faith"; Joe Christmas's earliest memory is that of a "quiet and empty
corridor"; and the orphanage dietitian who has such a profound effect
on Joe's life, though she has nothing whatever to do with Lena, comes
to see her life as "straight and simple as a corridor with [Hines] sitting
at the end of it." Finally, Percy Grimm also comes to "see his life
opening before him, uncomplex and inescapable as a barren corridor."
Although the meanings are different and even contradictory in each
context, the literal and metaphoric corridors become a connecting link
among the four characters.

Hines and McEachern accost the dietitian and Bobbie Allen with
similar outbursts: " 'Answer me, Jezebel!' " and " 'Away, Jezebel!' ";
Percy Grimm's "certitude, the blind and untroubled faith in the right-
ness and infallibility of his actions" suggests nothing so much as the
faith of Lena Grove; Hightower and his bride-to-be make use of "a
hollow tree in which they left notes for one another," an innocent
anticipation of Christmas and Joanna, who "insisted on a place for
concealing notes, letters. It was in a hollow fence post below the
rotting stable"; and when Hightower says abjectly " 'So this is love. I
see,' " he repeats in delusion Christmas's ecstatic discovery: " 'Jesus.
Jesus. So this is it.' "

Lena and Joanna both discover their pregnancies at the same time,
"Just after Christmas"; if Joanna were in fact pregnant, she and Lena
would both give birth in August. Given the confusion by Mrs. Hines
and Lena herself as to who her baby really is and who is its father, it is
as if Lena has borne not her own child by Lucas Burch, but Joanna's by
Joe Christmas. The story of Lena's conception of her baby is also like
that of Milly Hines, while Joanna's grandfather, Calvin Burden, is a
more sympathetic McEachern, beating the loving God into his children. Byron's weekend treks into the country repeat those of Hightower's father, who was secretly "riding sixteen miles each Sunday to
preach in a small Presbyterian chapel back in the hills."

Characters are constantly replacing each other, moving into squares on the board reserved for someone else, or repeating unwittingly the behavior of an unknown antecedent. Expecting to find Lucas Burch, Lena discovers Byron Bunch at the mill; when Hightower enters Lena's cabin, hopeful of receiving some reward for his services, he also comes as a poor substitute for Lucas.

This kind of substitution results at times in a bitter irony. During the initial chase after Christmas, prior to his arrest in Mottstown, the sheriff and his men are led by bloodhounds to a Negro cabin where the scent of Christmas's shoes has guided them. With pistols drawn, expecting to encounter the dangerous black murderer, the sheriff "kicked open the door and sprang, pistol first, into the cabin. It contained a negro child. The child was stark naked and it sat in the cold ashes on the hearth, eating something." Returning to the cotton house where Christmas apparently exchanged shoes with the child's mother, the men find "one astonished and terrified field rat."

Through such a tissue of echoes and repetitions Faulkner draws the fragments of his novel together, yet he does so at a huge price, deliberately paid, in truth as well as power. For this kind of order is an imposed one; it does not emerge from the action of the novel, and it is seldom realized by the characters. Instead they are metaphoric orders devised by an ingenious narrator and made available only to the reader of the tale, not to the people who have lived those echoes. The order achieved here is in the realm of what Coleridge meant by fancy, not imagination: relationships are established simply as structural gestures, a poetic order imposed on unpoetic and scattered materials. No transformation through metaphor occurs; we are not led by the work into a knowledge of a new order of things previously unseen. On the contrary, our logical sense of the novel's disorder remains intact, and our poetic sense of its order points more to the cleverness of the novelist than to a new vision of reality.

The pressure of genuine metaphor welding together what is logically irrelevant, gives way here to less assertive simile, suggesting resemblance while remaining securely aware of the actual differences between things. As Murray Krieger writes, "The test of poetry is whether or not it solicits us to end in another way of apprehending, whether or not it builds intramural relations among its elements strong enough to transform its language into new meanings that create a system that can stand up on its own" (A Window to Criticism). The aim of Faulkner's fiction is to approach such a way of apprehending, to create from chaos orders of reality that assert not only the power of the poet's consciousness but propose an entirely new truth.

But in the many figurative links of *Light in August* the novelist seems to provide nothing more than an ostentatious display of his prowess, of the skill with which he controls the fragments of his work. This is wild and disordered existence, the technique implies, saved only by the writer's manipulations creating what is obviously an illusion of order. The triumph, if triumph there be, is his; and the consolations of form appear to be not quite authentic.

Occasionally, it is true, these links are imagined not by a superior, outside intelligence, but by the characters themselves, as when Hightower links Joe and Byron by believing that both, in their "immoral" activities, are being guided by the devil. Most of the examples in the novel of this kind of metaphoric connection, the characters' conscious creation of relationships unfounded in fact, occur toward the end of the book; and it may well be that this is calculated to express a growing power on the part of such characters to break out of the novel's heavy fatalism and create, with whatever degree of illusion, the terms of order. The relationships between Lena's baby and Christmas are of this kind: Mrs. Hines imagines that the baby is actually Joe, born again, with the stain of his past and his murder of Joanna momentarily redeemed; and Lena occasionally finds herself believing that Christmas is her baby's father. For most of the novel, however, order is an external achievement imposed with almost Joycean care on material that is itself quite mindless of the connections and relationships it is serving.

This elaborate use of metaphoric form, much more prevalent here than in any other Faulkner novel, is consistent with the heavy fatalism that dominates *Light in August*. Characters come alive only in the restricted possibilities of their pasts. Many are caught in the fixed patterns bestowed on them by ancestors; others discover quckly the need for such frozen models and fashion these for themselves, quickly transforming them into prisons as solid as if they were conceived in the blood.

"And this too is reserved for me," Byron Bunch thinks, pondering the fact that he must tell Lucas Burch he is now a father; and Hightower receives his new sense of vitality, of potency: "It would seem that this too was reserved for me. And this must be all." It is the narrator who mutters the grim refrain: "But it is not all. There is one thing more reserved for him." With nearly all the characters, even Burch, who can

envision the "Opponent" who moves them all like chessmen on the board, life is little more than what is "reserved" for them. It is as if all were designed and done with before hand, the events of a life waiting patiently, like chairs in a wood, for their proper owner to happen upon them.

Both the action of *Light in August* and its method of structure through image patterns suggest, on one level, nothing so much as an enormous trap. In his role as narrator Faulkner becomes a detached sovereign, composing from a distance a network of figurative schemes that the characters unwittingly perform. The rigid patterns they *have* chosen find their fitting echo in those metaphoric links only author and reader are aware of.

The genuine fragmentariness of the fictional material—Lena and Joanna, to choose one example, have in *fact* nothing to do with each other—is altered only by the writer's superior establishment of order-making links. In the same way, the characters of the novel learn that the only protection against reality is the acceptance of solid patterns, inherited or created, with which they can shield themselves.

But this is only part of *Light in August,* for at the center of the novel, in this respect as in all others, is Christmas. In the midst of imposed orders is the figure of the man who challenges and expands the limits of his own given narrative, who both accepts and revitalizes the myth bestowed on him by his crazed grandfather, enlarges it to the structure of that self he is in the process of creating. Given the extreme dubiousness of the origins of the myth and Christmas's creative drive to expand it, we discover that we are not dealing with myth at all but with its transformation into a fiction: the authority of myth is not superior to but identical with the living structure of a creating mind.

And so it is Christmas who frees the novel from the innumerable links in which it is imprisoned. He does this, not as Lena does, by being blind to the chaos against which pattern is conceived, but by living a life whose pattern, the black and the white, he can sustain only by exploding first one part of the duality, then the other. This is pattern *in process,* the Apollonian confirmed and annihilated by the Dionysian. Through the forces of Christmas, *Light in August* drives, as no other Faulkner novel before it, toward a new fictional status: toward the idea of a supreme fiction, the form that feeds on its own dissolution.

The product quality of narrative, the pattern that precedes consciousness, is delivered over to the processes of consciousness. Narrative does not predetermine but draws forth the inventiveness that must complete the fiction. The narrative of Christmas begins with the not very-well-founded assumptions of his grandfather, but becomes a dynamic questing for identity: a fiction which is supreme because it retains a given shape even as it dissolves into expanding configurations of meaning.

Light in August comes to us then as the most enigmatic of Faulkner's novels. In its presentation of characters who require nothing so much as the security of imprisoning pattern, in its own metaphoric ordering of typically fragmentary materials, the novel presents a narrow view of the potentialities of human consciousness—and even extends that view to society in the form of Jefferson. Yet at the center of the novel, as if he were a god-figure enduring his necessary crucifixion at the hands of those who must see less for fear that they will see more than they dare to comprehend, is Christmas. The novel demonstrates that the ranges of human imagination are terribly restricted—its fairest model, the small town that has merely learned to live peacefully with its division; yet it also contains a figure who pursues the limits of consciousness. Faced with Christmas's intolerable pressures toward vision, community can only absorb him into its crude logic, call him by the name of blackness, and kill him. Yet is he not at the same time comparable to [Wallace] Stevens's hero, who rises "because men wanted him to be"?

> Large in their largeness, beyond
> Their form, beyond their life, yet of themselves,
> Excluding by his largeness their defaults.
> ("Chocorua to Its Neighbor")

He is the victim of their fear of vision, yet in their memories—expanding those integers of black and white they thought they had understood—he is the man who endures "forever and ever."

Fathers in Faulkner
and *Light in August*

André Bleikasten

> *La mort du Père enlèvera à la littérature beaucoup de ses plaisirs.*
> *S'il n'y a plus de Père, à quoi bon raconter des histoires?*
>
> ROLAND BARTHES

Faulkner's father figures range from such well-meaning weaklings as Reverend Mr. Mahon (*Soldiers' Pay*) or Mr. Compson (*The Sound and the Fury*) to comic villains like the blandly predacious Anse Bundren (*As I Lay Dying*), from dour disciplinarians like McEachern (*Light in August*) and arrogant despots like Thomas Sutpen (*Absalom, Absalom!*) to venerable patriarchs like Virginius MacCallum (*Sartoris/Flags in the Dust*); and whether living or dead, present or absent, domineering or feckless, malevolent or benign, they loom large in most of his novels. There would be little point, however, in categorizing them or in looking for some father archetype, for what seems to be at issue in Faulkner's intricate family chronicles is not the father as a person (a character), nor even the father as genitor, as the actual begetter of sons and daughters, but rather the haunting question of fatherhood, in its psychoethical as well as in its wider cultural implications. Far from being confined to the performance of a parental role, fatherhood appears throughout Faulkner's work as a complex function, both private and public, a symbolic agency operating on various scales and levels and within various patterns, and to discuss it only in terms of blood kinship and family structure would be to miss much of its deeper significance.

From *The Fictional Father: Lacanian Readings of the Text*. © 1981 by the University of Massachusetts Press.

Pater Semper Incertus Est

An astronomer knows whether the moon is inhabited or not with about as much certainty as he knows who was his father, but not with so much certainty as he knows who was his mother.

GEORG CHRISTOPH LICHTENBERG

Paternity is problematical from the outset. If motherhood is a plain fact, a natural given of experience, fatherhood, as Faulkner's novels suggest time and again, is not. Of the former, childbearing and childbirth provide incontrovertible evidence; the latter is always a matter of conjecture, if not sheer speculation. Moreover, who the father is appears to be of little moment in terms of biological reproduction. For the generation and perpetuation of life all that is needed is the father's seed; the father himself is dispensable. As Fairchild points out in *Mosquitoes,* "A woman conceives: does she care afterwards whose seed it was? Not she." Lena Grove, the earthy mother figure in *Light in August,* is a case in point: she has set out on a long quest-journey to find Lucas Burch, the rascal who seduced her and made her pregnant, but what she is actually seeking is just a father for her child, and it is quite immaterial to her whether his name is Burch or Bunch. It is noteworthy in this respect that most of Faulkner's pregnant girls and women— Caddy Compson, Dewey Dell, Milly Hines, Lena Grove, Laverne Shumann, Eula Varner—are unwed, and that the husbands of those who eventually get married are seldom the natural fathers of their children. As a consequence, many of his characters never come to know the true identity of their genitor. Januarius Jones, for instance, the frantic womanizer of *Soldiers' Pay,* "might have claimed any number of possible fathers." Miss Quentin, Caddy's illegitimate daughter, is "fatherless nine months before her birth," and so is, quite literally, Joe Christmas, whose begetting causes the murder of his—Mexican or Negro?—father by Doc Hines. In *As I Lay Dying,* Darl taunts his half-brother Jewel, Addie's adulterine son, with the question, "Your mother was a horse, but who was your father, Jewel?" and his cruel question is echoed in *Pylon* by Jiggs's asking little Jack, Laverne's son by Shumann or Holmes, "Who's your old man today, kid?"

Faulkner's world abounds in orphans and bastards, and whenever we discover in his adolescent or adult characters an acute sense of lostness, whenever his novels dramatize a failure to establish an identity of one's own and to come to terms with reality, there are fair chances that the roots of the tragedy are to be sought in the bafflements, frustrations, anxieties, and resentments of a deprived and disturbed childhood. And among the fatherless and/or motherless we must include the Compson children as well as Joe Christmas: having both their parents does not prevent Quentin and Caddy from feeling forlorn and doomed.

Fatherlessness is not so much the absence of a relationship as a relationship to absence. Besides, it should be noted that in Faulkner's novels the father's absence always casts a real shadow, and that whenever the actual genitor is dead or missing, his role is taken over by some collateral relative—an elder brother or cousin, an uncle, a grandfather—or, as in Christmas's case, by a foster father. In Yoknapatawpha no one, not even an orphan, can escape paternal tutelage totally, and one may well wonder if, in the end, it makes any significant difference whether the fatherly functions are assumed by the actual begetter or a surrogate, for in a sense all fathers, the "real" ones as well as their substitutes, are more or less *outsiders,* representing, within the family, a power that transcends familial bonds, and, therefore, is vested with an authority by no means "natural" in the way a mother's is. As Ike, another of Faulkner's fatherless sons, realizes during his lengthy argument with McCaslin Edmonds in "The Bear," "even fathers and sons are no kin." What comes first is the self-enclosed intimacy of the primal, nuclear relationship of mother and child; as to the father, he will always be at some distance from his progeny. Mutual affection may sometimes reduce the distance; it never conquers it completely, and at some point in the child's development this sense of remoteness will inevitably turn into hostility. As Gail Hightower recalls the fears and anxieties of his desolate childhood, he comes to liken himself and his mother to "two small, weak beasts in a den, a cavern, into which now and then the father entered—that man who was a stranger to them both, a foreigner, almost a threat. He was more than a stranger; he was an enemy. He smelled differently from them. He spoke with a different voice, almost in different words, as though he dwelled by ordinary among different surroundings and in a different world."

FATHER AND SON

For the child, then, the father is first of all a stranger and an intruder, the one—or rather the *other*—whose arrival portends the fatal breakup of the dual unity of mother and child. Yet of all strangers he is beyond doubt the closest and the most familiar. What is more, even though in the child's experience the father comes after the mother and represents an unwelcome addition to and disruption of the primordial couple, it does not take him long to find out that the father has been there before he was and has possessed the mother before he did. As John T. Irwin notes, "In this rivalry with the father for the love of the mother, the son realizes that no matter how much the mother loves him, she loved the father *first*. Indeed, the son carries with him in the very fact of his own existence inescapable proof that she loved the father first and that the son comes second." Priority in time is one of the very sources of the father's power, and since time is irreversible (except in fantasy), it is to the son a continual reminder of how little power and freedom he can negotiate for himself.

Priority is what gives the father mastery over the son; one might add that it is also what makes his mastery fully legitimate. Uncertain as far as its biological foundation is concerned, fatherhood badly needs the support and sanction of a cultural community. Originally, father power is derived or delegated power, and only social consensus makes it into a rightful one. All authority is *established* authority, the more easily accepted and the more unanimously acknowledged as it proceeds from the unbroken continuity of a cultural tradition. Paternal authority, therefore, is the more firmly settled as time has erased its contingent and hypothetical origin and hallowed its prerogatives as an undisputable "natural" right.

From these issues are derived some of the manifold complexities and contradictions of the father-son relationship. As a figure invested with legitimate power, the father inspires fear and envy, but also commands respect; as a rival for the love of the mother, he provokes both hatred and a strong sense of guilt. Moreover, if we believe Freud, all of experience urges the son to take the father as his first model, his first *pattern:* the little boy "would like to grow like him and be like him, and take his place everywhere" ("Group Psychology and the Analysis of the Ego"). Indeed, the father is the very object of his first *identification;* and as several (but not all) of Freud's statements on the subject seem to suggest, this identification process may occur even earlier than the Oedipal crisis and precede any definite object-choice.

Yet, whatever the time of its occurrence in the son's libidinal development, identification with the father is marked from the very first by ambivalence, and, therefore, is bound to result in unconscious conflict during the phallic phase, when the wish to be like the father comes to coincide and collide with the desire to replace him with regard to the mother. Hatred is then at its most murderous, but, however fierce, it does not preclude a measure of love, since in the "complete" (positive and negative) Oedipus complex an ambivalent attitude persists toward both parents ("The Ego and the Id"). Which is to say that, contrary to the simplistic assumptions of vulgar Freudianism, the father-son relationship is reducible in none of its stages to mere antagonism. It is essential to remember, on the other hand, the crucial function which psychoanalysis assigns to the father in the dialectic of desire and law that, under normal circumstances, leads to the achievement of selfhood. In the Oedipal triangle the father appears as the obstacle to the fulfillment of the incestuous wish; he bars the son's access to the mother, yet by the same token he also forbids the mother exclusive possession of the son. He thus releases the latter from the constraints and tensions of the family circle, allows him to move on to other object-choices, and furthers his entry into the system of alliances which rules and regulates the wider world of human exchange. In prohibiting and preventing incest, the father indeed performs a major cultural function, especially if, as Lévi-Strauss argues, the universal incest taboo is to be understood as the very cornerstone of human society.

His, then, is primarily the role of interdictor, of legislator through whose authority the maintenance of the cultural order is ensured within— and without—the family. Not that he is himself the author of the law: what authority he possesses he owes to society and its traditions or, to put it in more structural terms, to the specific *place* which he comes to occupy within the family configuration in relation to mother and child—a place previously held by other fathers, now dead, and which he will have to yield in turn to his son, a place "marked in life by that which belongs to another order than life, that is to say, by tokens of recognition, by names" (Marie-Cecile and Edmond Ortigues, *Oedipe Africain,* my translation). At this point it becomes obvious again how far the paternal function transcends the individual existence of the biological father. Or we might say that what matters most in the last resort is not the living father so much as the dead father, not the real father so much as the *symbolic* father or what Jacques Lacan calls the "name-of-the-father," "the symbolic function which, since the dawn of historical time, has identified his person with the figure of the Law" (*Écrits*).

Whether Freud's theory of fatherhood and its structural reformulation by Lacan possess universal validity is of course debatable. Yet as far as the classical, father-focused, Western family is concerned, they offer extremely suggestive models of interpretation. My purpose, however, is not to "apply" these models to Faulkner and to approach his novels as literary illustrations of psychoanalytic concepts, as there is, on the one hand, no transparent and irrefutable discourse of science and truth, and, on the other hand, there is no shadowy, delusion-ridden discourse of literature. Rather, I would suggest, Freud's and Faulkner's texts are to be read as differential versions of common concerns and, perhaps, of a common quest for knowledge, the former attempting to articulate in theoretical terms what the latter is trying to express through the language of fiction.

With both, one might note, there is an abiding fascination with the question of fatherhood. Paternity is central to Freud's interpretation of the Oedipus complex, as well as to his account of the formation of the superego; it is central, too, in *Moses and Monotheism* and *Totem and Taboo,* his later, highly speculative essay on the origins of religion and culture. As to Faulkner, his interest in fatherhood is attested throughout his work from *Flags in the Dust/Sartoris* to *A Fable,* and in at least four of his major novels—*The Sound and the Fury, Light in August, Absalom, Absalom!, Go Down, Moses*—the father-son relationship is assuredly one of the crucial issues.

VÄTERDÄMMERUNG

Dead, but still with us, still with us, but dead.
DONALD BARTHELME, *The Dead Father*

Faulkner's life-long preoccupation with sons and fathers must have arisen out of the depths of some private need, yet it seems safe to assume that it was also related in many ways to the particular society into which he was born and in which he spent most of his life. Faulkner was a Southerner writing about his native land; his questionings and probings cannot be dissociated from the unique context of Southern culture and Southern history. Southern society was almost from the outset a family-centered society. Indeed, in the Old South the patriarchal family typified to a large extent the proper relations between ruler and ruled and so supplied the primal model for social organization and political government. Father and master in one, the slave-holding planter of the prewar South was the source and locus of power: as paterfamilias, he claimed full authority over wife and children; as "massa," he felt entitled to demand filial subservience from his slaves. He thus presided over an extended family, white and black, and, as Eugene D. Genovese has demonstrated persuasively in his reevaluation of Southern slave society, this sense of extended family came to inform the whole network of race and class relations (*Roll, Jordan Roll: The World the Slaves Made*). The planters, it is true, were only a minority, and one should beware of oversimplification: the social order of the antebellum South was more complex and more fluid than well-established stereotypes would have us believe. Yet the plantation system conditioned all of Southern life, and the patriarchal and paternalistic values of the ruling class permeated Southern society at large. Whether paternalism mitigated the evil of slavery will long remain a matter of dispute among historians, but there can be no question that the father metaphor played a major role in the rhetoric of white male power, nor can it be denied that it had become a key concept—or rather a key fantasy—in the ideology of the South.

The Väterdämmerung set in after the Civil War, when the socioeconomic foundations of autocratic father rule began at last to crumble. The defeat of the Confederacy meant the end of slavery. Paternalism no doubt survived for many years among the remnants of the plantation system, and so did the patriarchal family structure till the early decades of the twentieth century. But the lordly father image associated with the planter ideal had become an image of the past. In the impoverished South of the Reconstruction years, fathers surely had as many responsibilities as ever, and their tradition-hallowed authority allowed them to keep control over the family. In the upper classes, however, their field of power had shrunk irretrievably. Compared to that of their predecessors, theirs was indeed a diminished role and one they must have filled the more self-consciously as they could not help but feel dwarfed by the formidable ghosts of their forefathers.

Out of the nostalgic memories of a lost world and out of the nightmare of a lost war, an imaginary South had arisen, as if to obliterate the real one—a collective mirage in which the old Cavalier legend blended into the Confederate myth born from the exploits of Lee, Jackson, Stuart, Forrest, and all the lesser heroes who had bravely fought and died for the Southern cause. And out of this compelling mirage grew Southern Shintoism and its wistful rituals. Probably nowhere else in America, not even in New England, was the ancestor ever held in so much reverence as he then was in the South, nor had he ever been such a powerful and omnipresent phantom.

Fatherland had become a haunted and haunting ghostland, and so the Southern father image was bound to become a divided one, at least in those families—generally of the upper middle-class—that had a sense of continuity and tradition. On the one hand, there was the glorious ancestor, the idolized dead father, safely enshrined in myth, intact and intangible in his godlike remoteness and the more indestructible for being timeless; on the other hand, the human, all too human, progenitor, the hopelessly prosaic real father, born into a time and place in which there was no longer use for the dazzling deeds of heroic gentlemen. How, then, could he be expected to serve as a model to his son? And with whom was the son most likely to identify in his youthful search for an ideal self if not his grandfather or his great-grandfather?

WHITE FATHER, BLACK SON

All religions are in essence systems of cruelty.
FRIEDRICH NIETZSCHE, *On the Genealogy
of Morals*

In *Sartoris* as well as in *The Sound and the Fury* and *As I Lay Dying,* Faulkner dramatized conflicts within a single family; in *Light in August* he seems to have been much more concerned with individuals in their relationship to society at large, and it is quite significant that in this novel all the major characters are at once aliens to the community of Jefferson and solitary figures without normal family ties. Yet their alienation from the community does not mean that they are estranged totally from its values. Indeed, all of them—with the possible exception of Lena Grove, who seems to exist in a space of her own—have absorbed and internalized these values so well that their conflict with society is always a war on two fronts, a war both without and within. That *Light in August* is a novel about alienation *from* society and its horrendous costs in violence and suffering is obvious enough; one should not forget, however, that it is as much—if not more deeply— concerned with the various forms of alienation inflicted on individuals *by* society.

It will not do, then, to reduce Faulkner's outsiders to more or less criminal deviates from the communal norm. Their minds have been patterned by their cultural environment; no matter how distorted, their mental categories and moral standards are those of their fellow citizens, the more inescapably so because in the closed, intolerant society in which they have to live no viable alternative is at hand. And in many ways they are representatives of that society. Not that any of the novel's protagonists can be identified with the average member of a given social or ethnic group (Faulkner's realism is a realism of extremes, not of averages). Eccentrics they are, yet each of them may be said to dramatize some essential aspect of the rural South in the early decades of the twentieth century. Thus, Gail Hightower embodies its obsessive involvement with a romanticized past, while Joanna Burden, the shunned "nigger lover," appears as an obverse reflection of its sexual and racial fantasies as well as of its puritanical sense of guilt. As to Christmas, the outcast par excellence, what makes him supremely significant is not at all his supposedly mixed blood, but his divided self, for it is through the splitting of his psyche, through the deadly combat between his "white" and "black" self-images that he comes to stand as a starkly truthful symbol of the tensions and contradictions of Southern society.

At the same time, however, Christmas is also a living challenge to his culture and its value system. Of the two identities available to him, he chooses neither, and what bewilders and infuriates the community more than anything else is precisely his stubborn refusal to meet its expectations, to conform to its standards, to act either as a "nigger" or a white man. Identity, in the world of *Light in August,* is above all a social imperative: people are required to fit into established classes and categories and to confirm through their normalized behavior the arbitrary divisions and hierarchies upon whose maintenance the very survival of the existing social arrangement depends. Those who cannot or will not fit must be expelled, therefore, from the body of society: Hightower and Miss Burden, the minor offenders, are relegated to the outskirts of Jefferson; Christmas, in punishment for his crimes, is castrated and killed.

Scapegoats are recurrent figures in Faulkner's fiction, yet in no other of his novels (except *A Fable*) does the putting to death of an outcast so strongly suggest the religious dimensions of sacrificial murder. In *Light in August* Faulkner resorts once again to Christian symbolism, but the way in which he uses it is far more complex and ambiguous than critics have been willing to acknowledge. Little insight is gained by calling Christmas an "inverted Christ" and leaving it at that. In fact, the analogies with Christ serve as much to emphasize the character's essential duality: just as he is both "white" and "black," he is both Christ and Antichrist—symbol of radical innocence in his agony and death as well as an emblem of extreme guilt.

Furthermore, Faulkner's tragic (rather than purely ironic) version of the Christ myth is given additional significance through its association with the novel's sexual and racial issues. Officially, Christmas's crime is the rape and murder of a white woman by a black man, and as soon as he has been identified as a Negro, no further proof is needed to establish his guilt. So he must die, and it is noteworthy that the circumstances of his death are a reverse repetition of his misdeeds: the killer is killed, and the rapist castrated. More than ruthless retaliation is involved, however, and there are other debts to be paid. The guilt Christmas is made to expiate is not only his; it is also the guilt unconsciously projected and discharged upon him by the whole community.

What does Christmas stand for in his role of pharmakos? On what "other scene" is the final act of his tragedy performed? At this juncture it may be helpful to recall briefly the psychoanalytic interpretation of Southern racism attempted by Joel Kovel (*White Racism: A Psychohistory*). In traditional, white-dominated Southern society, Kovel argues, the Oedipal conflict finds a kind of collective and institutionalized solution, with the white woman in the position of forbidden mother and the black man cast in the dual role of incestuous son and rival father: "the Southern white male simultaneously resolves both sides of the conflict by keeping the black man submissive, and by castrating him when submission fails. In both these situations—in the one symbolically, in the other directly—he is castrating the father, as he once wished to do, and also identifying with the father by castrating the son, as he once feared for himself." Cross identifications, cross projections, desire, hatred, and fear—these are precisely the feelings and mechanisms at work in the putting to death recounted in *Light in August*.

It will be remembered that Christmas's birth cost the lives of both his parents, that his first crime was the attempted murder of his foster father, and his second the rape and murder of a white woman. One might recall, too, that his story offers intriguing analogies with the Oedipus legend. Everything, in fact, urges us to see him as a new fictional avatar of the guilt-laden son figure. Yet if it is true that all sacrifices are to some extent symbolic reenacts of the primal patricide—the collective crime in which, according to Freud, all human societies originate—then Christmas also functions as a vicarious father. In the phantasmal scenario, his castration and murder represent the fulfillment and punishment of a single wish. As to Percy Grimm, the priestlike sacrificer, his chiasmal relationship to Christmas is at once that of father to son and of son to father. The places they occupy are exactly the same, but not their roles: while Christmas, the defenseless sufferer, is two victims in one, Grimm—in what we might call his *ambiviolence*—acts both as defiant son and avenging father.

Doubling is everywhere, and we even find it programmatically inscribed in Christmas's very name: "Joseph," the name of Christ's father, given to him by Doc Hines, the first surrogate father, the fanatical inquisitor who later turns out to be his grandfather; "Christ-(mas)," the name of Joseph's son, given to him in profane mockery by the dietitian, his starkly parodical nursing mother, and the other "sluts" of the orphanage. So Christmas is son and father through his name as well as through his sacrificial role, and in this respect, too, he is not unlike Christ, the divine Son partaking of the omnipotence of his heavenly Father. Yet the Christ he is associated with is the secularized, humanized Christ of the Transcendentalist tradition rather than the Messiah and Redeemer of orthodox Christianity, the humiliated and tortured son rather than Christ in his power and glory; and we might also note that his first name is not the name of Jesus' "real" father, but that of his pallid human substitute. In the father-son duality the emphasis falls obviously on the second term: Christmas is Christ in his passive suffering, in the agonies of his Passion, and his "resurrection" in the memory of myth is little more than the pathetic reminder of a crucifixion endlessly rebegun.

As to the ultimate addressee of the sacrificial message, he is neither a God of mercy nor even a God of justice. If one insists on relating him to the Judeo-Christian tradition, one might say that he is much closer to the jealous Jehovah of the Old Testament than to the Man-God of the Gospels. The metaphors designating him in *Light in August* as well as in some of Faulkner's other novels tell us quite clearly what he is: the "Opponent," the "Player," a power more infernal than celestial, manipulating men as though they were pawns or puppets and dragging them on inexorably toward disaster and death.

This God is a perverse and cruel tyrant, a terrible father. Conversely, the novel's paternal figures all act as if they were the duly mandated representatives of "the wrathful and retributive Throne." Never doubting that they have been personally chosen to carry out the Lord's will, Doc Hines and McEachern play God to Christmas. To the sons fall the duties and debts, to the fathers all the prerogatives of power. If the dominant social values in *Light in August* are those of the

white male, it is only in fatherhood that masculinity realizes its claim
to absolute mastery. In its social organization as well as in its ethos and
religion the early twentieth-century South portrayed by Faulkner is
still a patriarchy, although a debased one. Fathers control, command,
and punish. Small wonder that the God of Yoknapatawpha appears as
their magnified and idolized self-projection.

Of the inescapability and destructiveness of father power there is
no more chilling evidence than Christmas's tragedy. Yet in the lives of
Joanna Burden and Hightower its crippling effects are just as readily
discernible. Joanna's fate is sealed in early childhood, on the day when
her father takes her to the cedar grove where her grandfather and
half-brother are buried. At once spiritual testament and baptismal rite,
the father's pronouncement over the grandfather's grave is, in the
fullest sense of the term, a speech *act:* it loads the four-year-old Joanna
with the "burden" of her name and heritage, assigns her a place in the
chain of patrilineal succession as well as in the endless chain of the
doomed and damned, and so fixes the rigid pattern of her life. She will
try to break out of it, and her affair with Christmas may be seen as a
desperate attempt to reaffirm her repressed femininity in the face of her
puritanical fathers; in its third and final "phase," however, the latter
have regained complete possession of her mind and body, and she
eventually dies for having both obeyed and disobeyed their injunc-
tions. Acursed she is indeed, but the curse upon her is in fact nothing
but the searing trace of an evil utterance, male*diction.* Fatality, in
Faulkner, is clearly no metaphysical or theological issue, but a matter
rather, of language, of words said and heard, remembered or forgotten, and of the unpredictable ways in which they rebound and rever-
berate from generation to generation, trapping people in their tyrannous
echoes.

Hightower's is a different story. His prime obsession is not with
the "black shadow," but with "a single instant of darkness in which a
horse galloped and a gun crashed . . . [his] dead grandfather on the
instant of his death." To Hightower the ancestral past is not so much a
burden to be borne as a private theater in which he can play out every
night his heroic fantasies. Just like Joanna's, though, his destiny has been
preempted by the family ghosts. Born after what should have been his
life and death, dead before having been born, Hightower hovers in a
vacuum, outside time—"a shadowy figure among shadows, paradoxical." In providing him with an imaginary surrogate for manhood, his
compulsive, ritually repeated identification with the "apotheosis" of

the Confederate cavalryman grandfather has prevented him from achieving separate identity. Hightower's identification with the dead father is too passive to be acted out in suicide; it condemns him, however, to the absurd condition of death-in-life.

No matter how different the destinies of Hightower, Joanna Burden, and Joe Christmas, they resemble one another in that they are all determined by patrilineal filiation, and what strikes us again as decisive is the relationship to a figure more remote than the actual father. This holds true for Joanna and Hightower, who are both inheritors of a family tradition, but also for Christmas, the foundling, the seemingly rootless orphan. For he, too, has a grandfather, and it is Doc Hines' heinous, petrifying gaze that fixes and fractures his self and points the way to disaster. Christmas's early childhood is overshadowed by dead parents and a living grandfather, while Hightower's and Joanna's are by living parents and a dead grandfather. In none of these cases does the mother play an active part. Christmas's mother died in childbed, Hightower's wasted away in helpless frustration, and about Joanna's all we are told is that she was Nathaniel Burden's second wife and had been sent for by him like an item out of a mail order catalogue. As to the fathers, their sour-faced stolidity stands in revealing contrast to the raw ebullience of their own progenitors. For all their fierce puritanism, Joanna's and Hightower's grandfathers were by no means contemptors of life; they avidly grasped what it could offer and, much like Colonel Sartoris or Jason Lycurgus Compson, they had been shaped in the heroic mold of pioneers and warriors. Hines surely does not belong with them, yet in his demonic turbulence he strikes us as an obscenely caricatural reminder of their militant faith and, in relation to Christmas, his are indeed the godlike privileges of ancestral power.

If Christianity is the religion of the saving son, there is little Christianity in the society portrayed in *Light in August*. Neither is the patriarchal religion of Yoknapatawpha County that of the Old Testament. No convenant has sealed the mutual recognition of father and son, no angel stops Percy Grimm from killing Christmas. Grimm himself is the "angel"—an avenging angel with a butcher knife. And, contrary to the crucifixion of Jesus, the putting to death of the sacrificial victim serves no redemptive purpose. What we have here is patriarchy at its crudest and most savage: a system of self-perpetuating violence and cruelty, based on endless cumulation of guilt and endless repetition of revenge. Christmas dies in payment of a debt, but the debt is not discharged nor can it be. *Les dieux ont soif.*

The Reified Reader: *Light in August*

Carolyn Porter

> *But the spectacle is not identifiable with mere gazing, even combined with hearing. It is that which escapes the activity of men, that which escapes reconsideration and correction by their work.*
>
> GUY DEBORD

As the critical record demonstrates, we respond to the maddening puzzle of *Absalom, Absalom!* most often in one of the two ways suggested by Mr. Compson's response to the equally maddening puzzle of Sutpen's life: "It's just incredible," he complains, "It just does not explain. Or perhaps that's it: they don't explain and we are not supposed to know." The effort to explain leads to detective work. "Something is missing," as Mr. Compson put it, "you bring them [the characters and their acts] together in the proportions called for" by the "chemical formula," but "nothing happens; you reread, tedious and intent, poring, making sure that you have forgotten nothing, made no miscalculation . . . and again nothing happens." In particular, the effort to verify Quentin's knowledge about Bon has led to some elaborate poring over the text, "tedious and intent," in the effort to find that something which is missing. But even when the effort to explain takes on more judicious proportions, to order and comprehend the tragic dimensions of Sutpen's story, it cannot finally account for the telling of that story except by an appeal to imagination's superiority over reality— which amounts in the end to confessing that we are not supposed to know. On this view, Quentin and Shreve deliver up a "poem of the act of the mind in the act of finding what will suffice." No doubt

From *Seeing and Being: The Plight of the Participant Observer in Emerson, James, Adams, and Faulkner.* © 1981 by Carolyn Porter. Wesleyan University Press, 1981.

they do. No reader can fail to notice that Quentin and Shreve create both the richest and the most convincing version of the story. But it is not sufficient to assert that they succeed because they use their imaginations more energetically than Rosa or Mr. Compson. We need to ask why they are able to do so, and to call upon the transcendental imagination is merely to restate the question, not to answer it. In effect this appeal to the imagination represents the reader's romantic transcendence, while the detective's response reflects his insistence on neutral objectivity, both of which postures, as it happens, Sutpen embodies and ought to contaminate. The options available to the reader are apparently exhausted by Walter Slatoff's frank admission that we are not supposed to know, not because the imagination accounts for what reason fails to explain, but because Faulkner couldn't bring himself to work it all out. I would suggest that none of these responses is finally appropriate, because the novel's strategy is designed to block both subjective and objective escape hatches from history as the stream of event. Nor does Faulkner's novel reflect any final and irremediable incoherence in his own narrative procedures; rather, it reveals the incoherence and contradictions within the society he portrays, as well as in the society he addresses. In short, though I would agree with Cleanth Brooks's staunch insistence that the novel forms a coherent whole, I would support this claim on different grounds.

In order to understand Faulkner's strategy in *Absalom, Absalom!* we need to look first at the narrative experiments which led up to it. I wish to suggest that from *The Sound and the Fury* through *Absalom, Absalom!* Faulkner develops increasingly complex strategies for undermining the reader's detached contemplative stance. After describing the general direction of this development, I want to focus on *Light in August,* where its thematic implications become clear. . . .

The Sound and the Fury is actually Faulkner's simplest experiment in terms of technical conception. In its original form, without the appendix, the novel asks the reader to inhabit four successive points of view in order to construct for himself the story of the Compson family. The final section, moreover, offers a retroactive perspective on the events recorded which, while it may not present a single, privileged vision of the world of the novel, at least allows us to integrate all that we have seen from a single, detached point of view. *As I Lay Dying* is conceptually more complex. Instead of a gradually emerging group of characters set against a gradually emerging background, we have a field of interacting figures recurrently emerging out of a flux. Never allowed to settle for long into any character's consciousness, frustrated in our endeavor to form an image of more than passing instants, we are less confronted with the world of the novel than pulled through it along with the Bundrens. The novel imitates life not by re-creating the world in the form of a painting, but by re-creating experience as a flow of consciousness in which some images vividly remain to haunt us, but no sense of foreground and background is secure.

In *Light in August,* Faulkner combines the interior monologue with an omniscient narrator and expands the scope of his fiction from the family to the town. Here the reader's disorientation derives from the multiplicity of plot lines rather than from the multiple perspectives of the earlier novels. While *As I Lay Dying* resists our desire for the single, fixable perspective of illusionist space by forcing us through a rapidly paced substitution of one point of view for another, *Light in August* resists the same desire by refusing to allow us to follow any single action through to its completion. Each story necessitates another, until plot lines seem to spread out indefinitely. Moreover, we are set down in medias res, so that as we move forward in time, we double back further and further into the past. In *Light in August,* it becomes clear that Faulkner's manipulation of perspective is intimately involved with his interest in time. If we compare this novel with *The Sound and the Fury,* we can begin to see the relation between time and perspective.

In *The Sound and the Fury,* time is an explicit issue for Quentin Compson, who begins his last day by twisting the hands off the face of his watch. But time remains more an explicit thematic concern than an implicit means of coercing the reader. Within each section of the novel, a single perspective is developed through which we must fill in the events of the past. But once we begin to assemble the patches of time past revealed in the opening section, we are already engaged in the most complex activity the novel demands of us. Difficult though this task is, the stable and detached perspective afforded by the final section makes it possible to put the pieces of this puzzle together. Although *The Sound and the Fury* is the sort of puzzle capable of more than one solution, more than one assembled form, it is nonetheless a puzzle that can be assembled.

Light in August, on the other hand, while it makes the issue of perspective thematically explicit in the figure of Gail Hightower, the willfully detached observer seated behind his window, implicitly manipulates the reader by casting the omniscient narrator in the role of roaming listener and interpreter. That is, Faulkner refuses us a single, fixed perspective here—not by placing us in several minds successively, but by moving us from one place and time to another as the narrator focuses his attention on one character's story only to turn away to another's. The novel's first three chapters both initiate and illustrate this strategy at work. Faulkner turns from Lena, now in sight of Jefferson at the end of chapter 1, to Byron's memories of Joe Christmas's arrival in Jefferson at the beginning of chapter 2. Not until we are five pages into the chapter do we meet Brown, the man whom we would expect the author to introduce in the next episode of a book which, so far, seems to be centrally concerned with Lena Grove. So while confusion between Bunch and Burch leads Lena to expect Burch to be at the mill when she arrives, the reader, for the same reason, expects a comic plot to develop. Instead, he is introduced to a new character, Joe Christmas, whose story seems utterly irrelevant. By virtue of his name, however, Christmas cannot be a minor character, so the reader adjusts his expectations to encompass the possibility of tragedy, only to meet in chapter 3 still another character, Gail Hightower, whose relationship to Lena and Christmas must now be established somehow. From the outset, in short, the novel disrupts any expectations of a unified plot structure. This strategy is further complicated by the demand it makes on the narrator to give each character a past.

In *The Sound and the Fury*, the present consists of three days whose events are less important as episodes in plot development than as retrospective references to events in the past, references which serve primarily to establish relations between the two. The world of the present introduced in the opening section is provided with a past in the course of the novel, and the appendix Faulkner later composed for Cowley's edition of his works merely expands this history into the past and the future; in either case the past functions to deepen the meaning and elaborate the significance of these present events. Sartre was right when he argued that this novel has no future, because its present consists in events conceived not as acts with as-yet-undetermined future consequences, but as consequences already determined by as-yet-unrevealed previous events. As we read *The Sound and the Fury*, we are pulled forward not by the desire to see what happens next, but by the need to understand why this is happening now. In *Light in August*, the narrative pull encompasses both of these needs, a point which may be demonstrated by looking at the way the two novels begin.

Our confusion at the opening of *The Sound and the Fury* derives from the uncertain meaning of the word "Caddy." We must first learn its literal reference in the present, and eventually its symbolic reference to the past. Once this is done, however, the scene takes on both clarity and significance. The opening pages of *Light in August,* on the other hand, locate us in a world in motion, and present us not with a present scene whose meaning is fleshed out fully once we learn its relationship to the past, but with a moving present capable of leading us virtually anywhere. Lena Grove's quest to find the father of her unborn child, precisely by virtue of its apparent hopelessness, promises to carry us on an endless journey. The novel which proceeds from this beginning makes good on this promise; its plots proliferate at an alarming rate. But while forcing us to attend to the question of what will happen next in a present always moving forward, Faulkner also meets the demand which grows more urgent as this present grows more complex, the demand to fill in the history of the characters whose actions we witness. The reader's need to explain the present events by reference to their history, therefore, coexists (by no means peacefully) with his need to keep up with them as they pull him forward into an indeterminate future.

In *Light in August,* then, Faulkner denies not merely the ultimate validity of a detached perspective as he did in *The Sound and the Fury,* but the very possibility of one. For in *Light in August,* any fixed perspective we may hope to gain is disrupted by time's unceasing flow. In other words, the reader is compelled to order time while it is moving. I want now to explain more fully how and why Faulkner forces the reader of *Light in August* to engage in this struggle.

With the significant exceptions of Lena Grove and eventually Byron Bunch, the characters in *Light in August* are victims of ordering myths, of what Frank Kermode has called degenerate fictions (*The Sense of an Ending*). The townspeople of Jefferson form a community devoted not to fostering life, but to worshipping death, an attitude demonstrated by that "Protestant music" with its "quality stern and implacable, deliberate and without passion so much as immolation, pleading, asking, for not love, not life, forbidding it to others, demanding in sonorous tones death as though death were the boon." As the roles of Joanna Burden, McEachern, and Doc Hines make clear, the Protestant church supports and enforces that commitment to the rigid distinction between black and white which imprisons and destroys Joe Christmas. The church's capacity to redeem time, to provide that "peace in which to sin and be forgiven . . . is the life of man," derives from the paradigmatic fiction of time in which a kairos fills all time before and after with meaning, and thus redeems history by providing man with a place in it. But this fiction has, in Kermode's terms, regressed into myth; the Christian ordering of time has ossified into an institution committed to vengeance rather than to love, devoted to death rather than to life.

It is Gail Hightower, a man who has first retreated from life into the shelter of the church, and then from the church to his seat behind a window, who finally provides us with this vision of the church, and he does so in terms which help to explain why Faulkner has situated him behind that window as a willfully detached observer. In Hightower's final reverie, the church is seen as a failure not because of the "outward groping of those within it nor the inward groping of those without," but because of the "professionals who control it and who have removed the bells from its steeples." The bells which ring the hours, ordering man's days in accord with a redemptive organization of time, are gone. Developing the metaphor further, Faulkner describes all the world's steeples as "endless, without order, empty, symbolical, bleak, skypointed not with ecstasy or passion but in adjuration, threat and doom." Clearly, Faulkner's metaphor has sexual implications; the church is figured as "one of those barricades of the middle ages planted with dead and sharpened stakes," its power marshaled not in the service of procreation but of violence. By removing the bells from the steeples, the professionals have rendered the church impotent to foster life and peace, but all the more rigid and powerful in its ability to enforce its rule, to support the empty, symbolic distinctions which remain dogma.

But to notice the phallic imagery here is only to begin to see the significance of this conceit, for the bells' removal is an instance not only of the novel's elaborate concern with sexuality, but also of Faulkner's use of sound as a means of referring to that realm of continuing life which Lena Grove inhabits. The most obvious case of this technique is the insect noises which recur throughout the novel, particularly in reference to Hightower and Christmas. Faulkner reminds us repeatedly that "beyond the open window" at which Hightower sits, "the sound of insects has not ceased, not faltered," and that Joe Christmas moves through a world constantly alive with the sounds of crickets. Joe, of course, is cut off from this world, as is clear from the fact that the crickets keep "a little island of silence about him." Sounds are used to emphasize Joe's alienation not only from the natural world, but also from the human community, that community which, because the church has failed to unite it in the service of love and peace, has become devoted to death and vengeance. Sitting behind the open door of his cabin, Joe hears the "myriad sounds of . . . voices, murmurs, whispers: of trees, darkness, earth; people . . . which he had been conscious of all his life without knowing it, which were his life, thinking *God perhaps and me not knowing that too*."

These recurring sounds, then, reinforce our sense of the alienation from life from which Hightower, willingly, and Joe, unwillingly, suffer. But Faulkner's technique consists not merely in the use of "sound imagery." That is, I do not mean to say that all sounds in the novel "refer" in this way to a realm of continuing life; the case of the Protestant music makes this clear, for it is associated with death, not life. Rather, Faulkner is using certain sounds to signal the continuing life from which Joe is alienated as part of a more basic strategy which allies hearing itself with that temporal dimension which Lena Grove embodies, the continual present which sustains on-going life, but from which the church's ossified order has alienated it. This strategy can be seen in the novel's opening pages.

As Lena Grove sits beside the road watching Armstid's wagon approach, Faulkner describes the scene in terms of a contradiction between what she sees and what she hears:

> The sharp and brittle crack and clatter of its weathered and ungreased wood and metal is slow and terrific: a series of dry sluggish reports carrying for a half mile across the hot still pinewiney silence of the August afternoon. Though the mules plod in a steady and unflagging hypnosis, the vehicle does not seem to progress. It seems to hang suspended in the middle distance forever and forever, so infinitesimal is its progress.

Faulkner creates here the impression of constant change; the wagon's sound signals its motion, while its appearance is static. He is appealing to our predisposition to view immobility as permanence, but complicating our responses by attributing that permanence to motion itself. Characteristically, Lena allies herself with the wagon's sound, so that

> in the watching of it, the eye loses it as sight and sense drowsily merge and blend . . . so that at last, as though out of some trivial and unimportant region beyond even dis-

tance, the sound of it seems to come slow and terrific and without meaning, as though it were a ghost travelling a half mile ahead of its own shape.

As we know, Lena embodies the natural, procreative realm from which Joe is alienated and Hightower has fled. What I want to emphasize is that the way in which Faulkner establishes Lena's alliance with the earth's motion is by suspending her sight of the wagon ("the eye loses it") as he pursues her hearing ("the sound of it seems to come slow and terrific"). It is by locating Lena from the start in the "realm of hearing" that he makes her embody time's ceaseless progression.

Further, if we recall that the only order Lena seems to require is that minimal one indicated by her single metaphysical profundity, "My, my. A body does get around," the ease with which her hearing outstrips her seeing is hardly surprising. For Lena Grove—and this is essentially what undermines her credibility as a character while heightening her value as mythic force—exists in a perpetual present, a realm in which "time has not stopped" and never does, because Lena has no need to stand back and order her life in relation to time: she quite simply *is* time, understood as the "long monotonous succession of peaceful and undeviating changes from day to dark and dark to day."

By bringing us into the world of the novel through Lena's peculiar consciousness, then, Faulkner presents us with a world in motion, thereby introducing us to the task we must perform as we move through the novel to come. Beginning in medias res, recapitulating Lena's past in a brief four pages, and returning to the present where Lena has remained, waiting for the wagon, Faulkner then follows her progress until she comes in sight of the yellow column of smoke whose horrific source both we and Lena are eventually to discover. But as the novel proceeds, proliferating plots and characters, we are not content with concluding, as Lena does once again on the novel's last page, that "a body does get around." Unlike Lena Grove, we are incapable of inhabiting time without trying to order it. Set down in medias res, we need to stand back and find a way of encompassing the horrifying events we must witness. In this respect, we share with Hightower a need to retreat into the role of viewer, to secure a vantage point from which to integrate events, stories, and characters into a formal unity and so confirm our detachment from them and their implications. And like Hightower, we are forced in the end to accept defeat.

In contrast to Lena, whose slow and steady progress never stops, Gail Hightower is a man who, as we are repeatedly told, "has not moved." Terrified by the "hot still rich maculate smell of the earth," Hightower has long since fled from it, "to walls, to artificial light." We need not review the details of his peculiar flight from life. For present purposes, what is important is the fact that his flight from "the harsh gale of living" has finally taken the form of a withdrawal behind his window. The view framed by that window, however, is peculiar indeed. Hightower sits here not to look out on the living world itself, but to await a vision of the instant of his grandfather's death. He no longer looks at his sign, "his monument," and "he does not actually see the trees beneath and through which he watches the street," for he is waiting to see his grandfather and his troops "sweep past like a tide whose crest is jagged with the wild heads of horses," an event occurring each evening at "that instant when all light has failed out of the sky and it would be night save for that faint light which daygranaried leaf and grass blade reluctant suspire." Appealing to photosynthesis, Faulkner makes leaf and blade suspire, breathing out their stored-up light to produce "a little light on earth though night itself has come." For some light there must be, if the ghosts are to be seen. In the only full description we are given of Hightower's daily epiphany, the contrast between sight and hearing provides Faulkner with the means to indicate both the unreality of what Hightower sees, and his nonetheless adamant belief in its reality. The ghosts "rush past . . . with tumult and soundless yelling" and are gone as "the dust . . . fades away into the night which has fully come." And yet Hightower still believes they are there, because "it seems to him that he still hears them." Hightower's detached contemplative stance affords him the most encompassing vision afforded anyone in the novel, but his vantage point is irremediably contaminated by its focus on the dead rather than the living.

It is only the "steady shrilling of insects and the monotonous sound of Byron's voice" which persists in relating Hightower tenuously to the living world beyond his window. It is Byron Bunch—the single major character in the novel who allows himself to break free of the regulated order by which he has protected himself from sin and responsibility—who brings to Hightower's ears the news of Lena and Joe, and who eventually ushers Joe's mother into Hightower's house and seeks his aid when Lena needs a doctor. In short, it is because of Byron's habit of visiting and talking with Hightower that he eventually finds himself again involved with the living, hearing "the treble shouts of the generations," a participant in that world of birth and death from which he has fled.

If we return now to Hightower's final reverie, we will find Faulkner revealing through Hightower why any vision which promises to encompass events and redeem time is doomed to failure. As Hightower watches himself, in mounting horror, act out his life, the "wheel of thinking turns on" and he is forced to realize that he is responsible for his wife's death, that even by becoming his dead grandfather "on the instant of his death" he has not been able to remove himself from the burden of membership in the human community, since even if he *has* become his grandfather, he is still "the debaucher and murderer of his grandson's wife." Having been drawn into the events going on outside his window, Hightower is now forced to confront what his entire life has been devoted to denying—his participation in the world of the living, with all the responsibility this entails.

When he first nears this realization, the wheel of thinking "begins to slow" and he "seems to watch himself among faces, always among, enclosed and surrounded by, faces." Hightower's vision now takes the form of a "halo . . . full of faces." The wheel of thinking which becomes a halo is the complex vehicle for a metaphor whose tenor includes "all the faces he has ever seen." As wheel, the vehicle moves ceaselessly; as halo it appears to be static. The wheel/halo is Faulkner's version of Keat's urn, itself by this time translated from an emblem of Lena's eternal motion into both a womb and a tomb. For a moment, it seems that the faces "are peaceful, as though they have escaped into an apotheosis," but this peaceful vision breaks down, and for a reason similar to that which made Keats's urn turn into a "Cold Pastoral": death and historical time reassert their dominion. Joe's face is not clear, and as Hightower looks at it, he sees why: "It is two faces which seem to strive . . . to free themselves one from the other," the faces of Christmas and Percy Grimm. Significantly, these faces strive "not of themselves striving or desiring it . . . *but because of the motion and desire of the wheel itself*" (my italics). It is, then, the motion of time itself, signaled at the novel's outset by the sound of the wagon's wheels, and now by the wheel of time itself eternally moving, which both demands and resists the effort to conceive a vision which will organize time within a redemptive vision.

We can now see why the "freed voices" of those singing the Protestant hymns assume "the shapes and attitudes of crucifixions, ecstatic, solemn, and profound." Like Joe Christmas, when his body is described as "a post or a tower upon which the sentient part of him mused like a hermit, contemplative and remote with ecstasy and selfcrucifixion," those within the church are imprisoned by a degenerate fiction and thereby cut off from each other and from life's motion. In other words, those trapped within this order mirror the man forced to live outside it because of their common alienation from each other and from that "peace in which to sin and be forgiven . . . is the life of man." Joe Christmas and Percy Grimm are bound to each other in their common and unwitting enactment of a devotion to death. This is what Hightower understands when, foreseeing Joe's lynching, he thinks, "they will do it gladly, gladly" because "to pity him would be to admit selfdoubt and to hope for and need pity themselves."

Yet when Christmas is finally indeed crucified, whatever the citizens of Jefferson say to each other by way of ritual celebration, Faulkner apotheosizes him. He rises "soaring into their memories" to become a face "musing, quiet, steadfast, not fading," while the siren screams on, mounting toward its "unbelievable crescendo, passing out of the realm of hearing." To transcend the realm of hearing is to die; and in an unredeemed world, to die is to join the ranks of "all the living who ever lived, wailing still like lost children among the cold and terrible stars." Those whose voices assume the "shapes of crucifixions" then, adhere to a dead faith which severs them from all the living who ever lived, and these voices therefore remain "unheeded." In other words, the bells having been removed from the steeples, the church has come to represent not merely a retreat from life, but a citadel from which the human race itself, the living as well as the dead, has been exiled.

Hightower's vision reflects the larger struggle of both reader and narrator, the struggle to appropriate the ceaseless flow of time into an ordered fiction within which man can find meaning. This struggle is necessitated by the relationship between the past and the continuing present in the novel. From the moment we encounter Lena sitting in the ditch to the final moment in which the furniture salesman relates his comic story to his wife, time pushes forward, seeming never to stop despite the lengthy flashbacks into the past. Faulkner's strategy in maintaining time's flow can be most readily explained in terms of Henri Bergson's concept of memory as automatically preservative. According to Bergson, the "past . . . is necessarily automatically preserved." The present is a "certain interval of duration" like a sentence now being pronounced. Our attention spans the interval defined by the sentence, which can be elongated or shortened, "like the interval between the two points of a compass." The interval represented by one sentence can be stretched to include two by a change in punctuation. Accordingly, "an attention which could be extended indefinitely would embrace, along with the preceding sentence, all the anterior phrases of the lecture and the events which preceded the lecture, and as large a portion of what we call our past as desired." The present, therefore, is a function of the extent of our "attention to life." The distinction between the present and the past is a result of our apparent inability to sustain that attention; the present becomes past only when it no longer commands our immediate interest. If we did not have to channel our attention toward the future, if our attention to life were not repeatedly interrupted by the urgencies dictated by the practical concern of accomplishing our particular ends, our present would include our "entire past history . . . not as instantaneity, not like a cluster of simultaneous parts, but as something continually present which would also be something continually moving," something, in short, not unlike Lena Grove (*A Study in Metaphysics: The Creative Mind,* trans. Mabelle L. Andison). Further, it is this continually moving present which Faulkner takes pains to sustain throughout the novel.

For example, the paragraph leading into Joe's history, which constitutes the longest foray into the past if not the deepest penetration of it, works primarily on the principle that memory is not a system of pigeonholes, but simply a part of the flow of our consciousness, that attention to life from which we are artificially alienated. Accordingly, "memory believes before knowing remembers," because memory represents that intuitive awareness, that attention to life which never wanes but is only interrupted, so that knowing, intelligence, must remember, must search for and select those moments from the past which it deems relevant to the present. "Memory . . . believes longer than recollects, longer than knowing even wonders," and so represents a sustained subterranean flow, fundamentally unaffected by the interruptions imposed from above by the contingencies of survival. Accordingly, Faulkner modulates into the past without interrupting the flow of the present by referring the shift to a dimension which includes both past and present within the ceaseless flux of duration. He not only introduces the shift in this way, but repeats his appeal to memory as an enduring aspect of the present like a refrain throughout the following chapters, reinforcing our sense of the fundamental continuity of time.

Consequently, as the present of the novel flows on into an indeterminate future, we move simultaneously farther and farther into the past until, with Hightower's final reverie, we reach a point before the Civil War. Moving farther into the past while at the same time moving ceaselessly on into the future, the novel appropriates larger and larger chunks of time into a structure which is constantly struggling to enfold them within a unified vision. The novel not only operates on this principle but calls attention to it by deliberately, as it were, biting off more than it seems able to chew. As time moves on and plots proliferate, the novel sets itself an enormous task of assimilation: as the structure expands to encompass a lengthening history within an ordered whole, that order is continually revealing itself as inadequate to the larger demands for meaning posed by the continuously moving present. Thus there is a mounting tension in the novel between time's ceaseless motion and our attempt to impose a structure large enough to give that motion a meaning, to humanize it.

Light in August, then, enacts a struggle for a unified form which will encompass the events it records, a redemptive vision which will compensate for the inadequacy of the church's degenerative fiction. But just as Hightower's tragic vision of the human community as continuous and whole fails to encompass and redeem the events he has witnessed, and this because the wheel of time keeps turning, so the tension between the flow of time and the human endeavor to impose a plot, a redemptive order, on that monotonous succession of day and night persists unrelieved. The novel as a whole seeks to redeem a diminished world by making Joe Christmas's death a kairos for which Hightower's vision can supply a context and reference, but fails ultimately because that world keeps on moving.

For the same reason, the reader must fail in his endeavor to find a fixed vantage point from which to integrate events, characters, and stories into an ordered whole, separate and detached from himself. Had Faulkner ended the novel with Hightower's final vision, this would not be so forcefully true. But by telling the story of Lena and Byron on the road out of Jefferson through an entirely new character, the furniture salesman, Faulkner reinforces the implications of time's incessant progression into the future. Lena Grove's story acts as both bracket and ellipsis, to enclose and relieve the tragedy of Joe Christmas, but also to extend and amplify its intensity. By virtue of her health, her communality, and the sheer humor of her simple responses to life, she acts as comic relief to an intensely horrifying drama; but by virtue of the persistent and endless motion she comes to embody, her story extends and sustains the horror it ostensibly circumscribes. In a sense, her statement, "My, my. A body does get around," is quite seriously a profound one.

What gives it a tragic profundity, in fact, is that the body which gets around under the name of Joe Christmas is a mysterious object in his own eyes. Cut off from both social and natural worlds, Joe exists in a state of sheer chronos. Detached from pure duration, yet "doomed with motion," he is alienated from his own body as well, a fact which becomes particularly evident at those points when he is able to watch his own physical behavior from a distance in "motionless . . . utterly contemplative" moments. Sitting in the dietitian's closet as a child, Joe seems "to be turned in upon himself, watching himself sweating, watching himself smear another worm of paste into his mouth which his stomach does not want." Again when McEachern beats him, Joe's body is described as "wood or stone; a post or a tower upon which the sentient part of him mused like a hermit, contemplative and remote with ecstasy and selfcrucifixion." Sometimes his detachment is accentuated by a difference in velocity between his mind's and his body's movement, as in the scene in Bobbie's room after everyone but Joe has left. Before the "wire ends of volition and sentience" connect, Joe lies watching the events above him unfold in a pure succession, flowing without punctuation until, as the wire ends approach each other, Faulkner begins to intersperse the events with the connective "then." As the prose moves out of italics, "thens" pile up, reflecting Joe's increasing ability to distinguish between one moment and the next. Even after volition and sentience reconnect, however, Joe's mind still moves more slowly than his body, so that "he was in the hall without having remembered passing through the door." Finally, after gulping down the whiskey, his mind moves faster than his body, which he has to "coax . . . along the hall, sliding it along one wall" as if it were a cumbersome trunk. Whether body or mind moves faster, Joe watches himself move, and continues to watch after he has "entered the street which was to run for fifteen years."

Eventually, the street runs "so fast that accepting . . . takes the place of knowing and believing." It runs so fast that Joe no sooner sees a future possibility—*"Something is going to happen to me. I am going to do something"*—than it has virtually become a past fact—"Maybe I have already done it." For Joe, the present constitutes something possible, "waiting to be done" because he views the present as already past. Bergson asserts that viewing the present as a system of possibles which anticipate a future reality entails a false determinism in which the present is spuriously imprinted with the pattern of a future whose outline is unforeseeable; Joe's predicament embodies precisely that fatalism which derives from the act of structuring the present as if it were past. According to Bergson, the possible is a concept applicable only to the past wherein we try to find the causes for the present and so posit sources for that present. But when we apply this operation to the relationship between present and future, we necessarily fail because the present can only become possible from the vantage point of the future. Joe really has no present here, because he has already imposed on it the pattern which will define the future. The contrast between Joe's and Lena's modes of anticipating the future is instructive. Lena's future and past are enfolded in a perpetual present, out of which she anticipates the future and recalls the past not as distinct states, each one causing the next, but as the indistinguishable phases of a continuous flow. Thus the feeling of being on the wagon, even of having been on the wagon, does not disrupt the present, but seems to flow out of it without a break in time. Joe's present, however, is here defined by a pattern imposed on it as if it were past, so that he does not, cannot really, anticipate the future, except as the reality already possible in, and therefore determined by, the present. Joe exists in and is doomed by a pattern imposed before it is ever actualized. If for Lena the world is open-ended and creatively evolving, for Joe "his own flesh as well as all space" is a "cage."

Cleanth Brooks has recently argued that "the influence of Bergson on Faulkner has been generally overestimated and . . . its importance . . . occasionally pushed to absurd lengths." Brooks's central point, I take it, is that "Faulkner did not need to be told by Bergson or anyone else that life involves motion," so that in general, "what Faulkner got from Bergson was essentially a confirmation from a respected philosopher, of something that he already knew," and could have learned from Saint Augustine or Sophocles. "Life has always been associated with motion," Brooks tells us, and the literary artist has always faced the problem posed by life's fluidity and the static nature of words. While I agree that Bergson's influence has been occasionally overestimated, I do not think it quite accurate to treat that influence as a confirmation of timeworn truths about life and art dating back to Sophocles. Brooks's attention to the eternal seems to have obscured his perception of the particular, for I can see no other reason for his professed ability to find "little in Faulkner's narrative treatment that can be certainly attributed to Bergson's infleunce" (*William Faulkner: Toward Yoknapatawpha and Beyond*).

For one thing, there is a notable similarity of imagery in the two writers. Bergson at one point compares the feeling of duration to the "unrolling of a spool" of thread, as one feels "himself coming little by little to the end of his span"; reversing his implications Bergson continues, "it is just as much a continual winding, like that of thread into a ball, for our past follows us, becoming larger and larger with the present it picks up on its way; and consciousness means memory." Later, he uses thread once again to figure duration, but this time as "a thread holding together the beads of a necklace." Faulkner's imagery is more successful, but aimed at a similar goal. He compares the wagon Lena awaits to "a shabby bead upon the mild red string of road," and the road, in turn, to "already measured thread being rewound onto a spool." The point here is not that Faulkner necessarily got such images from reading Bergson, however, but rather that Bergson had, in fact, "helped" him, as he later told Joan Williams. That help would appear to have made a difference particularly to the "narrative treatment" in *Light in August,* where the "unrolling of . . . duration" which Bergson describes as both "the unity of a movement which progresses" and "a multiplicity of states spreading out" is unmistakably evident in Faulkner's narrative structure. In addition to the narrative modulation into the past on the basis of a Bergsonian concept of memory, the use of Lena Grove as a vehicle for a continual present, and the adaptation of Bergson's defense of freedom into a means for depicting Christmas's fatalism, we should also note that Bergson may have suggested to Faulkner the value of hearing as a register for motion. In "The Perception of Change," Bergson remarks that "we have less difficulty in perceiving movement and change as independent realities if we appeal to the sense of hearing."

Questions of influence, as some recent critical excesses reveal, are likely to obfuscate what they should illuminate, and I am not finally concerned with assessing Bergson's influence on Faulkner. But even had Faulkner not repeatedly mentioned his debt to Bergson, *Light in August* would seem to demonstrate it incontrovertibly. That debt however, is not essentially a philosophical one; in this respect Brooks is right. Faulkner used Bergson—as he confessed to using other authors— not as a source for ideas, but as a resource for narrative tools. The distinction is important if we are to recognize that Faulkner went well beyond Bergson in developing the implications of the claim that life is motion. Bergson, after all, argued for free will as an intuited truth grounded in the durational nature of reality. No such conviction is apparent in *Light in August* where the only person who might be called free in Bergson's terms is Lena Grove, and her bovine imperviousness to the tragic events among which her body moves around with such enviable impunity renders doubtful any claim that Faulkner adopted Bergson's philosophical beliefs. Indeed, *Light in August* demonstrates in several ways the limitations of Bergson's conceptual framework.

Bergson proposed to counter modern philosophical empiricism by an appeal to a truer empiricism which would overcome the deterministic implications of Kant's legacy. However, the concept of duration on which Bergson relied to accomplish this task, though providing a powerful basis for attacking the static objectivism of the scientific materialist, landed Bergson swiftly in the idealist camp, despite his disclaimers on this score. Because duration is "psychological in essence," as Bergson himself states, it can easily be reduced to a defensive weapon by romantic idealism, allying itself with the organic and natural against the static and mechanical. As Lukács indicates, the Bergsonian reaction against Kantian rationalism cannot overcome reification, for it merely reconstitutes it in the form of a reified flux set over against a contemplative observer. So much Faulkner learned from his experiment in *Light in August*, where consciousness as memory must serve as the register of life's ceaseless motion. Christmas in particular reveals the implications of Bergson's view of time as motion, for Joe constitutes one of the most alienated men in modern literature. The point is that life's motion is asserted in this novel, and in terms which make the reader's task extremely difficult, but the continual present remains abstract. A contemplative observer seated Buddha-like behind a window looks down upon an alien world of motion, signaled by the sounds of insects. The "wheel of thinking" signals one abstract motion, the insects another. The problem here is that life's motion cannot outstrip the limits of abstraction so long as it is figured in terms of nature. That Faulkner understood this problem becomes clear in *Absalom, Absalom!*, where the duration previously grounded in nature and signaled by sound, becomes a stream of events grounded in history and represented by the sound of human voices.

The Strange Career of Joe Christmas

Eric J. Sundquist

> *I am invisible, understand, simply because people refuse to see me. Like the bodiless heads you see sometimes in circus sideshows, it is as though I have been surrounded by mirrors of hard, distorting glass. When they approach me they see only my surroundings, themselves, or figments of their imagination—indeed, everything and anything except me.*
>
> RALPH ELLISON, *Invisible Man*

Ellison's protagonist, speaking to us from behind the veils of his creation and from just beyond the stark visibility sanctioned in law, if not in fact, by *Brown* v. *Board of Education* in 1954, betrays an anguish in which acquiescence and attack are merged. The subtlety of that anguish and the long accumulation of power on which it depends are prefigured in one of the epigraphs Ellison chooses for *Invisible Man* (1952), one that also looms in monstrous proportion behind *Light in August* (1932). In citing Captain Delano's perplexed question, "What has cast such a shadow upon you?" while deleting Benito Cereno's stunned reply, "The Negro," Ellison winds the explosive power of silence in Melville's tale one notch tighter and renders the ambiguous protest of his own narrative all the more invisible and threatening. The century that falls between the publication of *Benito Cereno* (1855) and the Supreme Court decision casts a shadow the American nation quite certainly has not yet escaped, a shadow, just as certainly, that some can never know except, perhaps, by radical acts of imaginative sympathy. "You wonder whether you aren't simply a phantom in other people's minds," says Ellison's protagonist. "Say, a figure in a nightmare which the sleeper tries with all his strength to destroy." The extremities of

From *Faulkner: The House Divided.* © 1983 by the Johns Hopkins University Press, Baltimore/London.

psychological enslavement articulated in these passages from Ellison's prologue are penetrating and remarkable not only because they present a form of lived alienation few whites could ever understand but also because they embody—from the other side of the mirror, as it were—the frightening responsibility for that alienation by coming as close as possible to enclosing in one revealed image the burdens of black and white alike.

The single image enclosing (but never quite merging) those burdens constitutes the tragic center of Faulkner's major work, a center he may be said to have worked toward but only properly discovered in the early stages of a novel first entitled "Dark House" and ultimately *Light in August*. The discovery came with the introduction, into a story first devoted to a demented minister, of Joe Christmas, the character whose tragedy, Faulkner later said, was that "he didn't know what he was . . . which to me is the most tragic condition a man could find himself in—not to know what he is and to know that he will never know." To debate the relative tragedies of Joe Christmas and Ellison's protagonist is probably futile; suffice it to say here that Faulkner may be right and that in Joe Christmas he discovered a character whose tragedy was the most powerful and ambiguous he could conceive. Both the power and the ambiguity of Christmas, as well as the imaginative courage that compels *Light in August,* only appears in proper perspective, however, when we recall that Faulkner, in 1955, would distinguish Ellison from Richard Wright, who "wrote one good book . . . [then] stopped being a writer and became a Negro. Another one named Ellison," Faulkner told his audience in Japan, "has talent and so far he has managed to stay away from being first a Negro, he is still first a writer." It is hard to say, here, how much of either *Native Son* or *Invisible Man* Faulkner had absorbed; he may have felt their power deeply, as deeply as he felt the Supreme Court decision of 1954, which he rather reluctantly endorsed but also put into critical perspective by noting that it "came ninety years too late. In 1863 it was a victory. In 1954 it was a tragedy."

This is indeed a peculiar remark, and it is only tolerable (not to say understandable) if we keep in mind that Faulkner was born in 1897 and virtually grew up with the resurgence of Jim Crow. The "tragedy" Faulkner refers to is the only tragedy he could thoroughly imagine—the tragedy of the South that includes but, from the perspective of white Southerners, can never literally embody the tragedy of the Negro: certainly not literally, but perhaps by a figurative embodiment that so engulfs and subsumes the literal as to bring them into perilous union. The further tragedy that Faulkner's best work from *Light in August* through *Intruder in the Dust* sought to express lies precisely in what must be, what can only be imagined or felt but never fully lived; and it is in the simultaneous rhythms of repulsion and union, of hatred and embrace, so vividly carried to their extremities of contact and failed resolution in Faulkner's style, that his most visceral understanding of that tragedy is realized. Those rhythms, which readers have quite rightly (but often for the wrong or less relevant reasons) assumed to be distinctly "Southern," create and sustain an act of imaginative vision that has no parallel in modern American writing. They do so because they re-create a moral and psychological sympathy that is at once courageous and, as Faulkner often claimed, inadequate, a sympathy that pervades his major works of the 1930s and 40s, but whose paradoxical contours can best be felt, once again, by placing side by side his later assertions that the fulfillment of *Brown* v. *Board of Education* could come "maybe in three hundred years," because "in the long view, the Negro race will vanish in three hundred years by intermarriage."

These contours are familiar to readers of Faulkner's fiction, and particularly familiar to those acquainted with his much publicized comments on desegregation in the 1950s. They are worth bearing in mind here simply because it is easy to take them either too lightly (and thus divorce his fiction from the realities it constantly struggled to incorporate) or too seriously (and thus convict Faulkner of a lapse in moral vision) when, on the contrary, they must be understood to continue to express both a defiance and a tragic sympathy that is completed and extended by their powerful ability to bring into further focus those conflicts arising between a novelist's "private" imaginings and his "public" postures. In some cases, as the history of literary criticism and biography demonstrates, the fiction itself may give way to ideas that have arisen against an author's will or without his consent; in others, like that of Faulkner, an author's adamant claim that he is not "merely telling a story to show a symptom of a sociological background" must be acknowledged but also balanced against the probability that his material itself, if not his public declarations, will define conflicts that are simply beyond his control. Faulkner's notorious "go slow" attitudes toward desegregation diverged little from those of the country at large and were not far out of keeping with the language of the *Brown* decree of implementation in 1955 ("a prompt and reasonable start," "good faith compliance at the earliest practicable date," "with all deliberate speed"), whose ambiguity momentarily revived the shattered dreams of Southern segregationists. By the time Oxford, Mississippi, became the scene of an insurrection that C. Vann Woodward has called "the most serious challenge to the Union since the Civil War," Faulkner had been dead nearly three months. The bloody rioting that accompanied the enrollment of James Meredith at the University of Mississippi in the autumn of 1962 confirmed once again—this time despite a nationally televised plea from President Kennedy and with the equally public complicity of Mississippi's states-rights governor, Ross Barnett—that Faulkner's native state, historically a leader in legal and illegal segregation, was now more than ever no state at all but virtually a country within a country.

According to Joseph Blotner, Faulkner a few days before his death had attributed the violent opposition likely to arise against Meredith's impending enrollment to a minority of white supremacists whose children did not attend the university; this is largely true, and we must certainly assume that Faulkner would have been appalled by the "Battle of Oxford" (in Woodward's phrase) that took place on 1 October 1962. It had not been so clearly the case in 1956 when Faulkner, contemplating the rioting that accompanied Autherine Lucy's enrollment at the University of Alabama, wrote his famous *Life* magazine "Letter to the North" that "the first implication, and—to the Southerner—even promise, of force and violence was [not such rioting but] the Supreme Court decision itself." Yet it is exactly the wrenching division of loyalties—dramatized in Oxford a century after the Civil War, as though to magnify more than half a century's struggle to reenslave and reliberate Jim Crow—that had become and would remain Faulkner's life in the form we know it best: his fiction. Mississippi, at the time of Faulkner's death, as it had been throughout his life, was to some observers a country within a country within a country; that is, a closed society still fierce in its isolation within the often closed society of the South itself, which for over four years in reality and well over a hundred years in its own imagination remained a nation socially and psychologically outside the nation that enclosed it legally and physically. The ratio between Mississippi and the United States, like the ratio between Faulkner's public statements and his fiction, describes a state of precarious union, one by which the form of Faulkner's career must be measured and in which we may find the rudiments of an analogy pertinent to his fictional encounter with the continuing problem of American slavery. For the state of being, the state of mind that Ellison's protagonist expresses—containing as it does nearly hallucinating layers of psychological involvement and complicity between slave and master—is an exemplary representation of the further and fiercer enslavement of black within white, and of *white within black within white,* that Faulkner discovered in *Light in August* and confronted until his death on Colonel Falkner's birthday in 1962.

The shadow of "the Negro" that descends upon Melville's Benito Cereno had long been and would long remain the central metaphor of America's most visible and continuing outrage, one that describes a union of responsibility and fantasy in which shadow and object, like black and white, are so inseparably fused as to be meaningless without each other. It is a metaphor Faulkner employs relentlessly in *Light in August* and one whose psychological power Ellison, a few years before *Invisible Man,* had sensed when he wrote that a "ritualized ethic of discrimination" enforced on whites as well as blacks led Faulkner, among other Southern artists, to discover in the Negro "a symbol of his personal rebellion, his guilt and his repression of it" (*Shadow and Act*). More recently, Daniel Aaron has focused attention on the most striking of the glaring deficiencies and failures of direct confrontation in century's worth of literature on the Civil War—the marginal role of the people whom that war, as it progressed, came to be about. For most writers, Aaron points out, the black man was at best "an uncomfortable reminder of abandoned obligations, or a pestiferous shadow, emblematic of guilt and retribution," and even for Melville, Twain, Cable, and Faulkner, haunted though they were by racial nightmares, he "served primarily a symbolic function and seldom appeared from behind his various masks" (*The Unwritten War: American Writers and the Civil War*). Such "black invisibility," as Aaron rightly puts it, is not very surprising in a canon dominated in literary history by white authors; but it is not for that reason any less revealing of a conspicuous feature of Faulkner's fiction—that he seldom chose to meet the political and military realities of the war face-to-face but rather enveloped himself in the perhaps more profound realities of veiling myths, the twisting corridors of the *might have been,* the long agony of history lived and relived in retrospective fantasy. Most like Twain in this regard, he chose to measure the past dream by the present nightmare, measuring both as they conflicted and merged like black and white, shadow and self, in the tangled rhythms of fact and fiction.

To say that Faulkner first discovered the full burden of his central tragedy in the midst of writing *Light in August* is of course misleading; he had detected (without extending) it much earlier, certainly as early as *The Sound and the Fury,* in which Quentin Compson realizes "that a nigger is not a person so much as a form of behaviour; a sort of obverse reflection of the white people he lives among." The startling effect of this realization, which in retrospect appears to lead directly to Faulkner's major works of the next twenty years, comes into dramatic perspective in *Absalom, Absalom!,* in which Faulkner reimagines and redirects Quentin's dilemma and suicide with an obsessive historical fury, enclosing it within the more haunting, more feverish and far-reaching story of Sutpen's Hundred. It is not misleading, however, to imagine that Faulkner's own rereading of his first great novel in the context of his greatest would not have been possible without the extraordinary deepening of style and theme that *Light in August* afforded. Like the story that revolves around Joe Christmas, the story that revolves around Charles Bon was first entitled "Dark House," as though Faulkner had been moving toward the stunted, explosive encounter between Quentin and Henry Sutpen ever since Quentin's suicide, and had found his way through the mediating figure of Christmas, a figure neither black nor white who (as Faulkner would later say in a remark that also bears upon the case of Quentin Compson) "deliberately evicted himself from the human race because he didn't know which he was."

Quentin's realization that "nigger" is a form of behavior, an obverse reflection of the white people surrounding him, resembles the brooding comments of Ellison's invisible man in that it too articulates two separate and parallel, but mutually dependent, phenomena: first, that the impenetrable mask of "Negro," however it divides the theories of historians and novelists, springs from a political reality that inevitably overleaps its varied social, physiological, and customary justifications; and second, that this masking is hallucinatory to the extent that, from a white perspective, it manifests the interiorization of racial trauma that led Faulkner, among others, to recognize that "nigger" —like all such epithets and possibly in some instances no more or less than "Negro" or "black"—describes not a person but a projected image. We might well speak, then, of two masks, one covering the other, which in turn appears to cover the invisible. The second is a kind of masking Ellison rightly situates in a more universal context of diversionary social and political behavior that for him includes the examples of Benjamin Franklin, Ulysses, and Faulkner (who, for instance, posed as the "farmer") and finds to be motivated, in the case of the "dumb act" of the Negro, by "a profound rejection of the image created to usurp his identity," a rejection that makes possible "the secret of saying the 'yes' which accomplishes the expressive 'no' " (*Shadow and Act*). The first is a masking that grows out of a responsibility for, and confrontation with, the second; and it develops by the paradox that, the more strenuous and intricate the probing of oppressed by oppressor becomes, the more the black mask may become fixed until it seems a reflection of the white, distortion upon distortion in an endless recession of mirrored images.

Such a masking of masking, in fiction and in fact, may blur into near incoherence the very best of intentions, as in the case of a notorious remark in preface to a pioneering revisionist study of American slavery: "I have assumed that the slaves were merely ordinary human beings, that innately Negroes *are*, after all, only white men with black skins, nothing more, nothing less" (Kenneth M. Stampp, *The Peculiar Institution: Slavery in the Ante-Bellum South*). To be a white man with a black skin—one of the potential absurdities that *Invisible Man* explores, and one that Faulkner himself appeared to encourage when he remarked in 1958 that the Negro's "burden" is that "it will not suffice for him to think and act like just any white man: he must think and act like the best among white men"—is in some respects precisely the threat that has motivated most racist hysteria since the Civil War. But its most compelling and, as Faulkner saw in the 1930s, tragic dimension was revealed in the obverse absurdity: to be a black man with a white skin, to be a virtual caricature, not only of an inhuman social and political system, but also of what in some minds was the most menacing result of that system's abolition. That such a menace inevitably contained more fantasy than actuality is neither surprising nor mitigating; far from it, for it is precisely the hallucinating "possibility" of miscegenation, which in the white mind has often maniacally exceeded its grasp of the facts, that forms and propels the strange career of Joe Christmas. From one point of view it hardly matters that the evidence of Christmas's "black blood" boils down to the second-hand testimony of a circus owner who had employed his reputed father, and that we receive that testimony from Christmas's fanatical grandfather, who has murdered the father; what matters is the other point of view, the climate of fantasy in which the evidence, whichever way it may point, counts for little beside the suspicion that overwhelms and submerges it, repressing and distorting it at the same time.

Light in August is an extended meditation on this fantasy, extended by Faulkner's desire to work out every conceivable variation, on every level he could imagine, within the limits of one sustained narrative. But Faulkner's desperate infusion of form with theme in *Light in August* only releases the full power it holds, and only—like Christmas at his death—rises forever into our imaginations, when we recall that the novel appeared approximately at the crest of a forty-year wave of Jim Crow laws that grew in part out of a threatened economy, in part out of increasingly vocal demands for black equality during and after World War I, and in greater part out of reawakened racist fears that had, at least in contrast, simmered restlessly for a generation between Reconstruction and the twentieth century. To be more exact, they grew out of the Supreme Court's decision in favor of the doctrine of "separate but equal" in *Plessy* v. *Ferguson* (1896)—a decision that rested the burden of its argument on a case involving a "Negro" who was "seven-eighths white" and could pass as white. Those years, which more or less encompass the lives of Joe Christmas, Quentin Compson, and Ike McCaslin, belong to Faulkner, who became a major novelist over the same period of time but did so by reminding us how old the new fears were, how little they had changed, and how long they were likely to last.

In probing those fears as they generate the turbulence of *Light in August,* let us risk citing one more remark by the Faulkner of the 1950s. Drawing an analogy for a University of Virginia audience between unassimilated blacks as "second-class citizens" and unassimilated dogs among a population of cats (or vice versa), Faulkner qualified his belief that, for "peaceful coexistence," it must be one way or the other (either first-class or second-class, "either all cats or all dogs") by adding that "perhaps the Negro is not yet capable of more than second-class citizenship. His tragedy may be that so far he is competent for equality only in the ratio of his white blood." Faulkner went on to qualify this qualification, just as on other occasions he made it clear that he thought the issue of "blood" was irrelevant; and it should be unnecessary by now to add that nothing is to be gained by accusing Faulkner of blatant racism. His analogy here rescues itself from embarrassment by mixing dogs with cats (rather than dogs with people), but in doing so it brings to mind the examples of the seemingly marginal, yet finally indispensable, animal analogies Twain invokes in *Pudd'nhead Wilson* (1894), a world of cats who can "prove title" and "miserable dogs" and curs who cannot. "I wish I owned half of that dog," David

Wilson declares to an astonished group of blockheads when an "invisible dog" makes a howling racket, "because I would kill my half." This remark, of course, is fatal to Wilson's legal career, gets him branded a "pudd'nhead," and is only proved wise, not to say prophetic, when it is ultimately brought to bear upon the tragedy of the black-and-white, white-and-black "twins," Tom and Chambers.

There are numerous and abundantly evident points of contact between *Pudd'nhead Wilson* and *Light in August;* the one worth bearing in mind here is the resemblance between the lawyer Pudd'nhead Wilson and the lawyer Gavin Stevens, both of whom endorse a theory of "blood" behavior to account for the tragedy of each novel's central character. Twain's complete title has usually been recognized to be *The Tragedy of Pudd'nhead Wilson,* and one must assume that Twain, adding irony to irony in the novel that "changed itself from a farce to a tragedy" as it developed (not unlike *Plessy* v. *Ferguson,* first heard in Louisiana in 1892 and then pending before the Supreme Court), fully intended us to confront a legal and moral abyss when Wilson unmasks the white Negro Tom, convicts him of murdering his stepfather-owner, and ultimately gets him sold down river to offset the indebted estate of his original owner. From a position hopelessly outside the community of Dawson's Landing, Wilson heroically moves to its center and becomes public spokesman for, and executioner of, its deepest fears and hatreds, endorsing by further and more brutal implication the theory—held even by Tom's mother—that his various disgraces and misdeeds are the result of his blood: "It's de nigger in you, dat's what it is. Thirty-one parts o' you is white, en on'y one part nigger, en dat po' little one part is yo' *soul*." Because Roxy goes on to trace Tom's confusing but prestigious genealogy through his father, Colonel Cecil Burleigh Essex, to Captain John Smith, to Pocahontas, and to "a nigger king outen Africa," it has to be noted that Twain's irony, which continually slips back and forth between convention and creation, between social conditioning and blood, is more complicated than this condensed summary can indicate. Quite certainly it is more complicated than the theory of Joe Christmas's behavior on the day of his execution offered by attorney Gavin Stevens:

> But his blood would not be quiet, let him save it. It would
> not be either one or the other and let his body save himself.
> Because the black blood drove him first to the negro cabin.
> And then the white blood drove him out of there, as it was

the black blood which snatched up the pistol and the white blood which would not let him fire it. And it was the white blood which sent him to the minister. . . . And then the black blood failed him again, as it must have in crises all his life. He did not kill the minister. He merely struck him with the pistol and ran on and crouched behind that table and defied the black blood for the last time, as he had been defying it for thirty years. He crouched behind that over-turned table and let them shoot him to death.

Whether Faulkner had Twain's lawyer in mind when he created Gavin Stevens (whose role in *Intruder in the Dust* rather seems to support this possibility), we can only guess. But Stevens speaks, as Pudd'nhead Wilson does, in service of an unbearable anxiety that, because it constantly threatens to dissolve into anarchy both a social and a psychic structure, can only be contained by the simplest of theories—one that is necessarily rendered farcical by renouncing the dangerous complexities in the surrounding actions of the novel.

Like the "fiction of law and custom" that turns white Roxy and her even whiter son into "Negroes," the fiction of Joe Christmas's black blood—"I think I got some nigger blood in me," Christmas tells his first lover, Bobbie, "I don't know. I believe I have"—subsumes within it a burgeoning historical reality that cancels out what is undeniably *visible*. In his case the ascendancy of that fiction is doubled because, though the evidence is utterly doubtful, even to the point of the darkest of comedy—"If I'm not," Christmas tells his last lover, Joanna Burden, "damned if I haven't wasted a lot of time"—it overwhelms not only the community that destroys him but Christmas himself as well. The climate of fantasy that cancels out what is visible, what is "white," makes the sacrifice of Joe Christmas all the more necessary and haunting—necessary because the blasphemous visibility of violent social disorder must be met with greater violence in order to totalize its repression; haunting because the narrative that contains the tragedy of Christmas at a constant, precarious edge does so by merging its own fictions with his, as in the metaphor chosen to describe Christmas's full passage into "blackness" after his apparent murder of his stepfather, McEachern: "vanishing as he ran, vanishing upward from the head down as if he were running headfirst and laughing into something that was obliterating him like a picture in chalk being erased from a blackboard." This erasure, plunging Christmas into some fifteen years of life as a "Negro," must nevertheless be posed against its opposite, the more brilliant and potent metaphor Faulkner chooses to describe Christmas when, on the night before his murder of Joanna Burden, he bursts forth naked into the headlights of an approaching car: "He watched his body grow white out of the darkness like a kodak print emerging from the liquid. . . . 'White bastards!' he shouted. 'That's not the first of your bitches that ever saw.' "

The figure of the photographic negative is so apt that we may hardly notice it at first. What it offers is a figure of simultaneous concealment and revelation, a figure that marks with explosive precision, at a point of passing from one to the other, the ambiguity of Joe Christmas, who—like Jim Crow, yet with the doubled ironic pressure of already appearing to be what he must but cannot become—virtually is a *figure* rather than a person. He is at once a reminder (of the amalgamation of white fathers and black mothers during slavery) and a threat (of the amalgamation of black fathers and white mothers ever since); as a "white" man fathered by one apparently only slightly more "black" than he himself is, Joe Christmas passes not simply between two races but also between two conflicting, complementary forms of anxiety. As a monstrous figure embodying at once an image and its opposite, a full measure of equality and its absolute denial, Christmas at a psychological level is a literal embodiment of the uncanny; while at a sociological level he is an emblem of his country's heightening trauma, containing "within" himself the fantasized projection of a further, invisible country within. It is necessary, in suggesting that *Light in August* is the greatest American treatment of the problem of "passing," to bear in mind what is obvious—that it is written by a white man often slow to sort out his own doubts and confusions about Jim Crow; for the enslaving myth of racial hysteria in the twentieth century necessarily surrounds and contains "within" itself the literal horrors of slavery it refers to but suppresses at the same time. The paradox, in this respect, seems almost a simple one: not how can a black man be a white man, but how can a white man be a black man?

The literature of passing had become relatively common by the publication of *Light in August,* most prominently in gothic romances such as Cable's *The Grandissimes* (1880) and Chestnutt's *The House behind the Cedars* (1900), but one of its most penetrating expressions had appeared in James Weldon Johnson's *The Autobiography of an Ex-Coloured Man* (1912). Johnson's protagonist, embodying the struggle with invisibility that Faulkner and Ellison would only be able to approach from their contrary positions of visibility, succinctly depicts his first thoughts on discovering that he is no longer white but black: "I did indeed pass into another world. From that time I looked out through other eyes, my thoughts were coloured, my words dictated, my actions limited by one dominating, all pervading idea which constantly increased in force and weight until I finally realized in it a great, tangible fact." Although the novel is hardly Johnson's own autobiography, it acquires more force by posing as such and by offering testimony whose singular authority makes the frenzy of Faulkner's version all the more pointed and inevitable. The relevance of the *Autobiography*, whose hero more prosaically but certainly more convincingly passes back and forth between black and white, gains further power from the fact that Johnson once projected in his notebooks a novel to be entitled "The Sins of the Fathers," which was to involve unknowing incest between the white daughter and the bastard Negro son of a Southern planter, culminating in the accidental death of the son and the suicide of the guilty father. Thomas Dixon had already used the title and a very similar theme, and Faulkner, familiar with Dixon if not with Johnson, would later write nearly the same novel— namely, *Absalom, Absalom!* To reach the novel he never wrote, Johnson, like Faulkner, was moving from the twentieth century to the nineteenth, from Jim Crow to the slumbering nightmare out of which he had sprung. He was moving, then, toward a more historical understanding of the entangling myths of race that only the passing of several generations could make wholly visible; and he was doing so, as Joseph Skerrett points out, by dramatizing in the *Autobiography* the tragic strategy of true irony, which Kenneth Burke rightly insists is based on "a sense of fundamental kinship with the enemy, as one needs him, is indebted to him, is not merely outside him as an observer but contains him *within,* being consubstantial with him" (*A Rhetoric of Motives*).

It is worth focusing all the attention we can on the irony Burke describes, for like Faulkner's metaphor of the photograph and its negative it elucidates a "kinship"—in the actuality of blood, in the legalities and illegalities of "separate but equal," in the embraces and denials of racial hysteria—whose generative power permeates Faulkner's major works. In *Absalom, Absalom!* and *Go Down, Moses* Faulkner would expose, in flashes of released cultural anxiety, the draining intimacy of that kinship; but in *Light in August,* where the stark sensuality of the sexual encounters between Joe Christmas and Joanna

Burden is more shocking than intimate, kinship is continually denied. Although the entire novel strives prodigiously, in detail after detail, to connect its characters by merging their responsibilities and actions, and by embedding their lives within one another in almost ridiculous ways, the effect of such exertions is quite simply to render the endless analogous details superfluous and the embedded lives fruitless. No sooner are the stories of two or more characters brought together than they are torn away from one another, creating in the novel, as in the problem of race it maintains at an agonizing pitch, an energy of fusion and division in which opposites appear to be created neither by emotional merger nor by extreme alienation but rather by holding both in generative, ironic proximity. What Irving Howe says of the book's social, religious, and sexual levels—that they can be distinguished for the purpose of analysis but actually "work into one another as the materials of estrangement, the pressures that twist men apart"—expresses this paradoxical tension well and defines, moreover, the true torment of Christmas's invisibility: the explosive pressure of containing the invisible in the visible and, more to the point, the visible in the *in*visible.

The circle of bondage that Joe Christmas at first seems to have broken in murdering Joanna Burden only leads him fatefully back to his place of birth. In returning to Mottstown in the borrowed shoes of a Negro—"the black tide creeping up his legs, moving from his feet upward as death moves"—he has "made a circle and he is still inside of it." Having been carried by fate to what seems his last destination, Christmas is finally called by his true, schizophrenic name—the "white nigger"—and, as an anonymous narrator appropriately assuming the collective title of "they" tells us, he acts accordingly: "He never acted like either a nigger or a white man. That was it. That was what made folks so mad. For him to be a murderer and all dressed up and walking the town like he dared them to touch him, when he ought to have been skulking and hiding in the woods, muddy and dirty and running. It was like he never even knew he was a murderer, let alone a nigger too." Finally Christmas does "act like a nigger" and allows himself to be beaten and jailed, as though in brief anticipation of allowing himself to be shot and castrated, an act in which Gavin Stevens, we recall, would have us believe he "defied the black blood for the last time." The posture of Christmas in his seemingly insane passivity, fusing the contradictory tranquillities of Stowe's Uncle Tom and Nat Turner but in essence resembling neither, can be construed as a kind of psychological exhaustion motivated as much by the spent fury and defeat of his character in the novel's formal terms as in terms of any fully conscious (from his own point of view) or fully conceived (from Faulkner's point of view) ideological decision. This is not to say that his death—or its manner, or particularly its mode of presentation—is insignificant but, rather, that it must be viewed as representing a continuation of the formal crisis that Faulkner pursues frenetically throughout the book: the crisis of containing the dominant story of Joe Christmas *within* a book he threatens to tear into dispersed fragments and, consequently, of containing the novel's excessive physical and emotional violence *within* a meaningful and legitimately tragic structure.

The extreme ambiguity of Christmas's behavior on the streets of Mottstown and in Hightower's kitchen (whether or not he acts like a "nigger," and why, is a point we must return to) can only be approached in abstract terms for the very good reason that the intense pressure of the novel, which resembles classical tragedy insofar as it leads Faulkner to a precarious invocation of Fate, appears to have grown out of the unexpected eruption, into "another" story, of the character Joe Christmas. To describe this eruption as a return of the repressed, the sudden casting over a story of the South of its long, peculiar shadow, is appropriate but, in formal terms, inadequate; aside from the special case of Joanna Burden and Joe Christmas there does not exist in the novel the kind of psychological union (and its inevitable inversion) between master and slave that compels *Pudd'nhead Wilson* and *Benito Cereno*. In terms of composition Twain's novel, because it began as a farce about Siamese twins and ended as a brilliantly botched meditation on slavery and miscegenation, offers the best comparison, but it is bound in contrast to appear, as it were, more psychologically integrated. When Faulkner wrote to his editor, Ben Wasson, that *Light in August* "seems topheavy" because "this one is a novel: not an anecdote," he not only brought into perspective the work of his career up to that point but also indicated an important formal development. Growing out of the violent superficiality of *Sanctuary,* which had itself been reworked in terms of the struggle in *As I Lay Dying* with loving, antagonistic analogous form, the new novel represented a hybrid of the two in which Faulkner mastered the realism of form by seeming to surrender to something beyond his control. The many complaints voiced by readers that *Light in August* struggles desperately but fails to bring the story of Christmas even into contact with the story of Joanna Burden (and more notably the stories of Hightower and Hines, and most notably those of Byron Bunch and Lena Grove) are perfectly justified: perfectly, for how else can Christmas's strange career, as man and as symbol, he characterized? The plunging, ravaging appropriation of larger and larger blocks of historical material, the summoning of one after another approach toward and withdrawal from the strangle-hold of the past, leave Christmas no less mysterious than when he is discovered on the steps of the orphanage and christened with his blasphemous name.

It is not clear whether Faulkner thought the material devoted to Christmas or that not devoted to him was responsible for making the novel "topheavy," but it hardly matters. It is precisely these two bodies of material, like the body of Christmas himself, that express in tangled and repulsive contradiction the novel's precipitous achievement of the only union possible between form and theme, between black and white, between the community and its sacrificial object. The best critical comment on *Light in August* appears almost incidentally in a 1945 letter to Faulkner from Malcolm Cowley, who was then prepar-ing *The Portable Faulkner*. Although he declared *Light in August* "the best of your novels as novels," Cowley was frustrated because, while it seemed to him at first that the novel "dissolved too much into the three separate stories" of Lena, Hightower, and Christmas, he ulti-mately found that they were "too closely interwoven" to be pulled apart. "It would be easy for you to *write* Joe Christmas into a separate novel," Cowley remarked, "but the anthologist can't pick him out without leaving bits of his flesh hanging to Hightower and Lena." The suggestive brutality of Cowley's metaphor is no doubt equally inciden-tal (surely more so than his decision, with Faulkner's approval, to anthologize the story of Percy Grimm), but it is nonetheless telling; for it describes, first, the wrenching physical union between Christmas and his community that is violently longed for and realized, and with more than equal violence rejected, in the novel; and second, it de-scribes the formal union that drives into fusion with others the story of Christmas and yet leaves his story, like his self, isolated, naked, living nowhere and murdered everywhere.

The formal violence that is needed to include Christmas within the novel's plot (which is less a plot than a puzzle put together under the strain of forced analogy) is more evident in the single link between Christmas and Lena Grove, the character with whom the novel begins (as did Faulkner's composition) and ends, and whose story provides the frame and the filtered domestic warmth that makes Christmas's story all the more terribly ironic. The alienating contrast between Joe and Lena, who never meet except through the novel's relentless probing of mediated psychological union, has led Cleanth Brooks, with oxymoronic precision, to characterize *Light in August* as "a bloody and violent pastoral." More immediately, it led Faulkner to what is at once the most improbable, haunting, and necessary scene in the book. When she mistakes Lena's baby for her grandson, "Joey . . . my Milly's little boy," Mrs. Hines brings the anguish of Joe [Hines]-McEachern-Christmas into a heightened relief that is only surpassed by Lena's consequent confusing of Christmas himself with the child's father, Lucas Brown-Burch: "She [Mrs. Hines] keeps on talking about him like his pa was that . . . the one in jail, that Mr Christmas. She keeps on, and then I get mixed up and it's like sometimes I can't—like I'm mixed up too and I think that his pa is that Mr—Mr Christmas too—."

The union of Christmas and Lena exists only in—one might rather say, between—these two confusions about him as father and as son, a significant coupling because throughout the novel it is exactly the ambiguity of the filial relationship that determines the burden of his life. Moreover, and more importantly, it is also the relationship that is made to represent the trauma of the South in its acute sexual crisis—the threat that an invisible menace will become all too visible. Because the novel constantly raises the specter of miscegenation, that menace appears before us on every page, in nearly every line of Christmas's story with paradoxical clarity; but precisely for that reason—and even in spite of the vivid, lurid trysts of Joe and Joanna—we may forget, may want to forget what looms in the background of Christmas's life and his novel. Like the early illustrator of *Pudd'nhead Wilson* who either failed to read the book or was stricken by moral vertigo when he depicted the decidedly beautiful *white* Roxy as an Aunt Jemima figure, we may (certainly in the 1930s if not in the 1980s) simply not believe our eyes. The one doubtful and unverified fact of Christmas's existence that is responsible for Mrs. Hines's mad confusion (that he is the *son* of a "nigger") also sets in motion the menace unwittingly articulated in Lena's confusion (that the "nigger" will *father* a white woman's child) and compels Faulkner, on the verge of failing to bring his novel into any coherent focus, to risk a connection that is perfect to the very extent that it is the product of desperate fantasy. The power, as well as the necessity, of such a fantasy is the single feature that holds the fragmented, momentary crossings of plot in place and saves the novel from wasting every one of its passionate efforts at characterization. As he exists in this more extreme form of "passing" between worlds—from son of a "nigger" to "nigger" as white father—Christmas seems nearly a perverse caricature of white racial hysteria. Not so perverse, however, as the amendment to a typical "racial purity" bill introduced into the Virginia legislature in 1925 that would have required all citizens to register, with the state Bureau of Vital Statistics, all racial strains, however remote, that had ever entered their families; and not so hysterical as the climate of anxiety that led to the measure's rejection—because it was clear that many fine Virginians, living and dead, would be classed as Negroes.

That hysteria in part determines the elegantly distorted shape of the novel, shape determined (it might also be said) by the complementary pressure of containing Christmas, as character and as fantasy, who seems passively to bend the lives around him into a form capable of expressing his own, which in itself, if it is not nothing, is certainly left veiled and intangible. Irving Howe has noted that the "mulatto" excites in Faulkner "a pity so extreme as often to break past the limits of speech" and thus produces some of his "most intense, involuted and hysterical writing." Simply at the level of syntax this observation applies more exactly to *Absalom, Absalom!* and parts of *Go Down, Moses;* but it is with respect to the form of *Light in August,* which may in the end pose more interesting formal problems, and which in any event appears to have made the later novels possible, that the importance of Howe's claim must be judged. In the novel that turned Faulkner's career toward its greatest materials and their most significant expression, the crisis of blood works jointly with the crisis of form, both turning Faulkner back toward the 1860s in search of a solution, however partial and fragile, to the continuing crisis of history in the South.

By way of passing to a more explicit consideration of the problem of the novel's form, let us note again that the intersection of the three crises—of form, of blood, of history—lies in the embracing crisis of sexuality, which compels the confusions that bring Christmas and Lena into their first, fantastic moment of contact and which generates a second, more oblique but more conclusive one, the contact made in the mediating presence of Hightower when Christmas is lynched. Although Brooks has rightly insisted that Christmas's death is a "murder" rather than a lynching, I want to use the word with full deliberation in order to stress the climate of fantasy the book assumes and depends on for its power. In his 1929 study of lynching, dedicated to James Weldon Johnson, Walter White reported that the issue of sex "in the race problem and specifically in lynching is distorted by [a] conspiracy of semi-silence into an importance infinitely greater than the actual facts concerning it would justify." That conspiracy both results from and produces something of a willful blindness to what clearly exists (the historical fact of the rape of black women by white men during and after slavery) and a hallucinatory frenzy about what exists more in fantasy than in fact (the inexorable craving for and rape of white women by black men), thus making it nearly impossible, White noted, to elicit from many Southerners any kind of response on the subject but one of "berserk rage" (*Rope and Faggot: A Biography of Judge Lynch*).

There is no more need to point out that White's formulation is not intended to be definitive of an entire people than there is to add that it is true enough as an abstract representation, not of the South alone but of the entire nation that brought Jim Crow into visible existence, to warrant our attention. Before the character Christmas can bring these tensions and fears to their climactic expression in the outraged cry of his priestlike executioner, Percy Grimm—"Has every preacher and old maid in Jefferson taken their pants down to the yellowbellied son of a bitch?"—he must himself be made to represent, to embody from both sides of the mask, the distortions of feeling and fate that the crisis of sexuality can release. He does so in the long, long plunge into his past that Faulkner requires seven chapters (almost exactly the middle third of the book) to negotiate. The flashback of Joe's earlier life centers him "within" a novel pervaded by frames, by memories of memories, by stories embedded within stories embedded within stories; that is, it brings him, as the novel does each of its major characters, out of the resonant darkness of the past and into the slight but explosive moments of contact before communion breaks in denial by rendering formally visible his unknown or unrecognized being already *within* them.

As Christmas exists as a fantasy of black within white, he comes in the novel's action to inhabit and create the critical moments of the lives of others—fortuitously in the case of Joanna Burden, fatefully in the case of Doc Hines, tragically in the case of Hightower, by the gamble of tenuous analogy in the case of Lena Grove, and with apparently preordained justice in the case of Percy Grimm. Faulkner's surging narrative dislocations of time have received more attention than any other aspect of the novel, and rightly so, for they are all that can make dramatically plausible the lives of characters that are otherwise stunted by gorgeous but deadening obsessions. What is noticed less often is that the lives of those characters who most embody the life of Christmas as a racial fantasy (Joanna Burden, Hightower, Hines, Percy Grimm) are also the ones that Faulkner seems able to treat only by analogously disjointed plunges into the past. Once this is seen, however, we recognize as well that the shape of the novel is more distorted than ever. Aside from her functional act of childbearing, which reveals the potential contamination of Christmas as it appears and passes away in its most unnerving, because radically peripheral, form, Lena Grove serves simply and beautifully to frame and contain the violence of the novel; and Byron Bunch, the displaced narrator on whom much of the burden of Faulkner's story falls, appears hardly more than the medium of Lena's containment of that violence, which centers in Christmas and reaches back toward chapter one and forth toward chapter twenty-one through the subsidiary frame of Hightower's life. The book's symmetry, of course, is not perfect, and there is no particular reason to wish it were; for though we may object to the narrative's chaotic detours and its forcing into probability coincidence upon coincidence, particularly in the aftermath of Joanna Burden's murder, the possibility ought also be entertained that it is only those diversions from a single line of action—into the extended recapitulative histories of Hines, Hightower, and Grimm—that can make visible the complete alienation of Christmas in formal terms. In order to eventuate in its appropriate sacrificial function, the story of Christmas must set in motion the stories that surround his not so much by merging, but rather by colliding, with them. Joe Christmas must be both central and marginal, sacred and profane, galvanizing and menacing: he must momentarily release into the public horror of revealed story those distorted passions of a community that are otherwise hidden and suppressed.

In recognizing that *Light in August,* like *As I Lay Dying* before it and *Go Down, Moses* after it, contains four or five incipient novels, we need to note that Faulkner's psychological chronology works toward an approximation of life rather than the seamless web of "fiction." As Byron Bunch realizes of his own increasingly perilous involvement with Lena, *"it was like me, and her, and all the other folks that I had to get mixed up in it, were just a lot of words that never stood for anything, were not even us, while all the time what was us was going on and going on without even missing the lack of words."* This remark applies just as clearly and appropriately to Joe Christmas, who, like Addie in *As I Lay Dying,* almost willessly determines the shape of the stories that surround and impinge upon his own. The novel's expressed antagonisms between public and private, along with the attendant misunderstandings and hypocrisies they make possible, are realized in a narrative form whose rhetorical melodrama creates stories as they are needed, virtually at the moment they come into the action of being. Joanna Burden's story thus becomes "public" (as her life becomes meaningful) in the novel's terms by being expressively contained in Christmas's and released by her murder; the stories of Hines and Grimm, and the more significant depth of Hightower's, are similarly released by and into the public crisis precipitated by that murder and their own fated involvement in it. In an early scene that clarifies the degree to which *Light in August* represents an extension of the formal experiments of *As I Lay Dying,* the novel itself forecasts the form these expressions will take when Lena waits for a wagon that will take her to Jefferson. As the wagon approaches, "like already measured thread being rewound onto a spool . . . as though it were a ghost travelling a half a mile ahead of its own shape," Lena thinks to herself, *"it will be as if I were riding for a half mile before I even got into the wagon, before the wagon even got to where I was waiting, and . . . when the wagon is empty of me again it will go on for a half mile with me still in it."* There is no need to elaborate the way in which the novel, in story after story, in a recollective form that insists on the sudden and precarious violation of one life by others, gathers and rewinds the potentially random but critically connected threads of its lives. Any one of the characters might be compared to the wagon as a ghost traveling ahead of, and therefore determining, its own shape; they each "contain" already within themselves the lives that will be made manifest in strained momentary contact, and this containment, as well as the strain it expresses, is reflected in the visible, literal containment enacted by the novel's form.

In stressing that the issues of race and miscegenation are fully involved in the novel's form, there is no reason to suggest that this involvement is an explicitly causal one; *Light in August* might well have had a similar form without the ambiguity of Christmas's blood, without his being "Negro" at all. Obviously, though, it would not be the same novel, nor would it be capable of expressing with such haunting social and psychological complexity, with such power to contaminate and bring to crisis, the radical internalization of black within white. In this respect, the issue of blood, the epitome of the many spurious connections and analogies that fuse the novel's divergent lives, appears to be the only feature that rescues much of the narrative from a collapse into cascading, uncontrolled rhetoric. It does so by keeping that rhetoric at the tenuous edge of collapse and thereby measuring the fragility of the South's social and psychological order. Faulkner himself intimated the formal crisis the novel expresses when, in response to a question about the "style" of *Light in August,* he characteristically replied that he didn't "know much about style" but went on to speak vaguely of something "pushing inside him to get out." Since Joe Christmas says almost exactly the same thing of his contaminated blood, there is nothing to prevent us from saying that this something, bluntly, is the "nigger in him"—"nigger" not as blood, as enslaving memory, as the simultaneously feared and needed *other,* but as all of these, as the formal and psychological embodiment of a crisis that became even more acute in the life of Jim Crow than it had been in the second generation of slaves and masters Cash speaks of: "Negro entered into white man as profoundly as white man entered into Negro—subtly influencing every gesture, every word, every emotion and idea, every attitude" (*The Mind of the South*).

The form of Joe Christmas's early life, released in a flashback constituting a third of the novel and framed by his murder of Joanna Burden, is itself pervaded by stories within stories that enact in further significant detail the interiorization of lives with which the remainder of the novel struggles. The most important of those stories, the story of Joanna Burden's heritage as it is placed within the context of her sexual ravishing, bears almost the entire moral weight of the issue of miscegenation. It ties together the different religious zealotries of Christmas's two surrogate fathers, McEachern and Hines, and it is forced into more explicit genealogical parallel with that of his last figurative father, Hightower, both in its antebellum depth and in the aroused suspicion of "nigger-loving." Like the corncob rape of Temple Drake in *Sanctuary,* what we remember most—are perhaps most meant to remember—about *Light in August* is the violent sexuality of Joe and Joanna, whose analogous expression is the ecstasy of religious fanaticism. This analogous relationship is amplified as soon as we notice in turn that the story of Hines, representing the obverse merger of the two, has a function similar to the psychobiography of Popeye that Faulkner appended in his revisions of *Sanctuary.* Although it is not the ironic joke that the story of Popeye's childhood seems to be, the story of Christmas's fated origin, placed within that of the maniacal Hines, represents an excursion into religious naturalism that expands, but cannot possibly explain, the horror that has already been revealed.

Extending the naturalistic tragedy of *Pudd'nhead Wilson* by enveloping it in an aura of Calvinistic damnation, Faulkner creates for Joe Christmas the prominent place in the classic American tradition many readers have sensed he has. He does so, however, in a way that has seldom been taken into full account, for Hines's obsession with the "bitchery" of original sin, raised to an extreme pitch by the specter of miscegenation, brings into view a very peculiar strain of Southern racist thought. Among the many bizarre and scandalous efforts to justify white supremacy by evicting the Negro altogether from the human species (and surely something of a highpoint in centuries of "scholarly" and "scientific" research into the subject), the most notorious at the turn of the century were those of Charles Carroll, who argued in *The Negro a Beast* (1900) and *The Tempter of Eve* (1902) that Eve was seduced by an apelike Negro, not a serpent, and that the whole history of man's long fall from grace therefore derived from this original sin of bestial miscegenation. Such a distant tainting of white blood obviously raised questions answered only by a fanatical devotion that is more preposterous than its own germinal theory. It was a devotion the South was familiar with in less extravagant forms; and as we have seen in the case of *The Sound and the Fury*—and more particularly in the case of *Sanctuary,* where Popeye at several points is described with deliberate ambiguity as a "black man"—Faulkner had already begun developing a psychology of American original sin that would include its most troublesome, because undeniably "real," form— the mixing of white masters and black slaves. Faulkner invokes the hysteria of miscegenation as original sin only tangentially in *Light in August* (without further clarifying its broader historical import, as he would in *Absalom, Absalom!* and *Go Down, Moses*), but it is important to note that it, too, determines the form of Christmas's life by determining the form that the dependent crises of blood and sexuality take.

In the long act of narrative memory devoted to Christmas's life as he consciously knows it, both the resonant sexual terror of Joe and Joanna, which the whole novel strives to encompass and contain, and the "womansinning and bitchery" of Hines into which Faulkner's fascination with this terror eventually dissolves, are prefigured by an act of formal interiorization enveloping what may be the book's most preposterous and penetrating scene. In chapter eight, approximately in the middle of Christmas's story, his affair with Bobbie moves toward its violent climax—the apparent killing of McEachern—by moving first into the recent past. The chapter begins with Joe "passing swift as a shadow" down the rope he uses to escape his bedroom, and the next chapter begins with McEachern, the full power of his "bigotry and clairvoyance" turned on, recognizing Joe's shadow and following him to the dance. In between, we are carried back into a recollected account of Joe's affair with Bobbie, and in the middle of that account we are carried back to a peculiar moment earlier in Joe's life that is also framed on the one hand by his first surreptitious meeting with Bobbie and on the other by his physical attack on her when she reveals on that occasion that she is having her period and cannot make love. The brief flashback that interrupts the larger flashback, which interrupts yet larger flashbacks, is nothing less than a primitive act of sacrifice. Horrified by one of his adolescent friend's description of menstruation— "the temporary and abject helplessness of that which tantalised and frustrated desire; the smooth and superior shape in which volition dwelled doomed to be at stated and inescapable intervals victims of periodical filth"—Joe slaughters a sheep and kneels to it, "his hands in the yet warm blood of the dying beast, trembling, drymouthed, backglaring. Then he got over it, recovered." He does not forget what he has been told, but simply finds that he can "live with it, side by side with it." This strange act of purification, which is presented with little irony but which seems nonetheless flagrantly absurd, thematically recapitulates Joe's earliest memory (the parodic primal scene between the doctor and the dietitian); it refers more immediately back to his refusal of a sexual encounter with a black girl ("enclosed by the womanshe-negro," he is overcome by "something in him trying to get out, like when he had used to think of toothpaste"); and it points forward to his future sexual exploits—in which he will insist to lovers and whores alike that he is a Negro, through which the twisted passion of Joanna Burden will be released, and for which he will in the end be killed and castrated.

The scene of the sheep slaughter is not particularly well conceived, and it is typical of Faulkner's lapses into obfuscation at critical moments in his plotting of symbolic action. It has little of the sacrificial significance of the hunt in *Go Down, Moses* and cannot carry the burden Faulkner apparently wants it to unless we recognize the figurative function of the blood sacrifice. We should emphasize, in this regard, that the novel's focus on sexuality at its climactic moments represents both a furthering and a containing of the form of violence it continually refers to more obliquely—the violence of slavery and the racial hysteria, which either immediately or more remotely is dependent upon sexuality; that is, on "blood." The importance of this sacrificial scene thus lies in part in the fact, as René Girard has pointed out in a different context, that menstrual blood may easily be taken "as a physical representation of sexual violence," a representation whose "very fluidity gives form to the contagious nature of violence" (*Violence and the Sacred,* trans. Patrick Gregory). It is precisely such contagion that is rendered doubly powerful in the specter of miscegenation, the specter yoking violence with sexuality under whose aegis Joe Christmas is sacrificed in a violent denial of sexuality. The nature of that sacrifice requires further examination; but to see it clearly we must first see clearly the one union between two characters in *Light in August* that determines the warped shape of all the others: the relationship of Joe Christmas and Joanna Burden.

Their union is, of course, the book's center. It is a union of two masks, of mirror images (even in their names), that also parodies the possibility of real, loving union by reducing it to violent sex between a spinster living in "an old colonial mansion house" and a small-time hood living in its deserted "negro cabin." The enervating compulsion of their relationship arises as Faulkner, apparently striving to counter one myth, creates another that necessarily includes, extends, and makes more terrifying the first. For in countering the violent sexual desires of Christmas with the ever more frantic desire for violation he arouses in Joanna, Faulkner produces a psychological amalgamation that responds to the menace of physical amalgamation by internalizing it as a brutal struggle between conscious repression and unconscious eruption. As they exist in a bizarre replica of slave and master, enacting and passing between the South's own version of original sin and the contemporary threat it makes credible, Christmas and Joanna represent at a psychological level the tangle between *repression* and its failure that corresponds to the tangle between *oppression* and its failure at a social and political level. The fact that Joanna is a "nigger-loving" descendant of New Englanders is important to the extent that it reflects Southern accusations both before and after the war that the North endorsed miscegenation, and manifests in the mind of the South exactly that emancipation, in fact and in fantasy, which makes Christmas a monstrous figure; but this in turn is only fully dramatized when, once Joanna has been murdered, the community's antiabolitionist sentiments are forgotten and completely engulfed by racial hysteria. As the narrative puts it, she is killed "not by a negro but by Negro"; and when the community, hoping "that she had been ravished too," begins to "canvass about for someone to crucify," Joanna becomes more than anything else a "white woman," archetypically embodying Southern gynealotry and its concomitant "rape complex."

That complex, the result of an intense confusion between guilt and self-justification, has been analyzed by a number of social historians, but prior to Faulkner it achieved its most popularly significant (though far less interesting and complicated) expression in the racist novels of Thomas Dixon, which had a prominent place among the racist sociological literature that quickened the rebirth of Jim Crow. The climactic scene of *The Clansman: An Historical Romance of the Ku Klux Klan* (1905), for example, involves the rape of a white heroine by a black "animal": "A single tiger-spring, and the black claws of the beast sank into the soft white throat and she was still." In the wake of such moral horror and degradation, the girl and her mother commit suicide rather than face the public humiliation it entails. When Dixon's novel became *The Birth of a Nation* in 1915, the image of "the Negro as beast," long a stock figure in the South and elsewhere, was visibly fixed as the icon to which almost any justification of Jim Crow could ultimately be referred. Although the climate of hysteria that existed probably did not require it, the iconography received ample support, not just from obvious lunatics like Charles Carroll, but also from more respected commentators like William Hannibal Thomas, who dedicated *The American Negro: What He Was, What He Is, What He May Become* (1901) to "all American men and women of Negroid ancestry who have grown to the full stature of manhood and womanhood" but maintained, among other things, that "negro nature" is so "thoroughly imbruted with lascivious instincts" and "so craven and sensuous in every fibre of its being that a negro manhood with respect for chaste womanhood does not exist." After endorsing Thomas's views, the novelist Thomas Nelson Page added that, although the actions of lynch mobs are indeed shocking, there is a deeper shock "at the bottom of their ferocious rage—the shock which comes from the ravishing and butchering of their women and children." The problem arises, Page observed in a characteristic mixture of frenzy and delicacy, because the teaching of equality means but one thing "to the ignorant and brutal young Negro"—"the opportunity to enjoy, equally with white men, the privilege of cohabiting with white women" (*The Negro: The Southerner's Problem*).

Although there was considerable disagreement as to whether the "pure black" or the "mulatto" was most degenerate, and therefore most likely to violate white women, miscegenation was, at the height of Jim Crow, hardly seen as a serious solution. The point was nearly moot, however, since in the wake of *Plessy* v. *Ferguson* the "one-drop" rule prevailed in fact if not in every courtroom: as Thomas remarked, "a mass of white negroes would . . . merely add to an already dangerous social element," because "the variegated freedman would still be a negro in mind, soul, and body." This, of course, is Joe Christmas's problem. And in *Can the White Race Survive?*—like White's *Rope and Faggot,* also published in 1929, the year in which *Light in August* appears to be set—James D. Sayers picked up the old and still predominant argument that civilization would eventually be destroyed unless the "frightful cancer" of miscegenation was eradicated with a surgeon's knife wielded "vigorously and with a steady hand . . . before it gets so spread into [our] vitals that it cannot be rooted out." This, of course, is Percy Grimm's theory—not an uncommon one, either, even though the statistics on lynching, such as they were, showed that between 1900 and 1930 fewer than one sixth of the blacks lynched could actually be accused of rape. But "those who believe in the visibility of ghosts," wrote Frederick Douglass, "can easily see them," for race prejudice "creates the conditions necessary to its own existence" and "paints a hateful picture according to its own diseased imagination" ("The Color Line," *The Life and Writings of Frederick Douglass*).

This is nearly the language of Hawthorne, and as such it clarifies one aspect of the "romance" of race in the South and in the nation, clarifies it even more brutally when we recall that Dixon's white supremacy novels were subtitled *Romances.* No more appropriate term can be imagined, however, for *Romance* in this case brings together in the "diseased imagination" Douglass invoked a virulent nostalgia, the menace of sexual violation, and a twisted utopian vision, which, to say the least, make the Southern penchant for Walter Scott pale in comparison. Such a characterization perfectly describes Dixon's *The Leopard's Spots: A Romance of the White Man's Burden, 1865–1900* (1902), the language of whose preface is calculated to arouse fantasy—"It will be a century yet before people outside the South can be made to believe a literal statement of the history of these times. I have tried to write this book with the utmost restraint"—and whose abiding message is the threat of the "mongrel breed" articulated most vividly by the Reverend John Durham: "*In a Democracy you cannot build a nation inside a nation of two antagonistic races; and therefore the future American must be either an Anglo-Saxon or a Mulatto.*" The test of a man's belief in equality, Durham later asserts, is "giving his daughter to a Negro in marriage. . . . When she sinks with her mulatto children into the black abyss of Negroid life, then ask him!" That Dixon's "test" seems nearly a parody of the stock question hardly discredits its power; on the contrary, it reenforces the obvious continuity of Southern thought on its most elemental, visceral issue. The war transformed the Negro into a "Beast to be feared and guarded," wrote Dixon, and now, as then, "around this dusky figure every white man's soul was keeping its grim vigil."

That this "dusky figure," this shadow, is indeed a *figure* rather than a person is what generates the ambiguous power of Faulkner's own "romances" of race. It is in *Absalom, Absalom!* and *Go Down, Moses,* which like Dixon's romances spread across the entire history of the South, that the contagion of the racist imagination must be measured; but it is in *Light in August* that Faulkner found the key to the mysterious country of Yoknapatawpha by finding in Joe Christmas and Joanna Burden the climactic realization of a hysteria that had necessarily been building since Reconstruction. He found in Christmas the utter, alienating paradox of that contagion, and he found in Joanna Burden its gestating, enclosing receptacle. To put it in such sexual terms—thus literalizing the anxiety implicit in Cash's figurative assertion that "negro entered into white," as white had into Negro—is not at all unwarranted; for the complementary converse of Joe's repeated aversion to both black and white women ("the lightless hot wet primogenetive Female" that seems to enclose him "on all sides, even within him") is Joanna's nymphomania, which reaches its rhetorical climax in her frenzied erotic exclamation: "Negro! Negro! Negro!" By making Joanna a "nigger-lover" before making her a "nigger's lover," Faulkner deflected attention away from a more unsettling possibility he had already explored in the brilliant story "Dry September" (1931), in which the "rape" of a white Southern spinster by a black man is clearly suggested to be a product of her own diseased imagination. It may be that Faulkner found this possibility too dangerous to elaborate in *Light in August* and thus countered Joanna's explicit desire for violation with her New England abolitionism. As we have noted, however, it hardly matters; once she is murdered, she becomes as white and respectable and Southern as the communal hysteria requires.

In Joanna Burden's frenzied embodiment of a state of seizure that, with all the characteristics of released repression, expresses a direct counterpoint of the South's greatest fear, we also find an ironic emblem of the more far-reaching observation of James Weldon Johnson: "The South today stands panting and almost breathless from its exertions." Just as Joe has spent much of his life in a state of "physical outrage and spiritual denial," "trying to breathe into himself the dark odor, the dark and inscrutable thinking and being of negroes, with each suspiration trying to expel from himself the white blood and the white thinking and being," Joanna's correlative breathless exertions engulf and internalize him as the alien *other*—the invisible seed of black blood that should be, that *must be* mixed with her own. Their physical union enacts a "pantomime of violation," as Howe remarks, but it represents as well the vivid climax of the historical fantasy that created it. Entering the "gutter filth," the "sewer," the "bottomless morass," the "swamp," the "pit [of] the hot wild darkness" of Joanna's desire, Christmas enters the actualization of a fantasy that creates his life and leads to his death: "It seemed to him that he could see himself being hunted by white men at last into the black abyss which had been waiting, trying, for thirty years to drown him and into which now and at last he had actually entered." The surge of "pent black blood" that accompanies his execution, rushing "from out the slashed garments about his hips and loins . . . like a released breath," expresses the origin and end of racial violence as it is transformed from twisted fantasy into grim reality, as it is raised from visible menace into visible sacrifice. The medium of that transformation, the shocking sexuality of Joe and Joanna, bears all the fateful weight of inherited tragedy as their affair nears its conclusion, the two of them "peopled, as though from their loins, by a myriad ghosts of dead sins and delights, looking at one another's still and fading face, weary, spent, and indomitable." And her false pregnancy with his "bastard negro child," apparently the result of menopause, is the ironic culmination of the novel's romance of blood.

Maxwell Geismar is thus absolutely right, for the wrong reasons, to complain that the tragic union of "the Negro and the Female, the twin furies of Faulkner's deep southern Waste Land," leads to no redemption or proper catharsis in *Light in August,* but rather can express only "the world of human perversions whose precise nature is that they are also infantile emotions . . . the reflections of our early animal instincts which have been blocked and forced out of their normal channels of maturing" (*Writers in Crisis: The American Novel, 1925–40*). The failure of emotional catharsis in the mating of Joe and Joanna, because it holds in tension the adolescent rite of purification Joe performs and the greater communal effort at purification performed by Percy Grimm, makes further evident the infantilizing relationship between white and black, which in some respects the abolition of slavery could not eliminate but could only intensify. It is therefore essential that the brutal gothicism of *Light in August*—which grows out of a union among Calvinism, racism, and naturalism—be seen to derive from "infantile emotions," for it is these very emotions that require a (white) system of social and political convention to be justified on the basis of (black) primitive, animal, "natural" instincts. This has been the argument of every racist commentator from antebellum years through the twentieth century; it even lies behind the most disturbing aspects of Thomas Jefferson's thoughts on black slavery in *Notes on the State of Virginia* (1787). Troubled that emancipation might not be possible without the freed slave "staining the blood of his master," Jefferson was driven to an analogy whose apparent absurdity nevertheless had the sanction of centuries of thought on the origins of blacks. Situating his understanding of the natural difference between black and white in the neoclassical language of beauty, Jefferson noted that the superiority of elegant, symmetrical white physiognomy was proved even by the Negroes' own "judgment in favour of whites, declared by their preference of them, as uniformly as is the preference of the Oranootan for the black woman over those of his own species."

Jefferson did not bother, or could not bring himself, to unpack the details of this explosive analogy. Perhaps for him, rumored to be the father of mulatto children—and so portrayed in one of the first novels by a black American, William Wells Brown's *Clotel, or, The President's Daughter* (1853)—the emotions were too complex and personal to admit of extended analysis. His assertion in any event, as Winthrop Jordan remarks, recapitulates with a "geyser of libidinal energy" some of the "major tenets of the American racial complex" and at the same time may transfer to others his own repressed "desires, unacceptable and inadmissible to his society and to his higher self," thereby draining them "of their intolerable immediacy" (*White over Black: American Attitudes toward the Negro, 1550–1812*). Such a dramatic transfer of repressed desire to its complementary paranoid fantasy describes rather exactly the progression of racist thought from slavery through the equally tenuous justifications of Jim Crow. The myth of excessive virility and lust in the Negro as "beast" derived historically from his presumed direct descent from the ape, most commonly the orangutan; and Jefferson's minor displacement of that theory of descent into more liberal distinctions—the black man preferring the white woman, as orangutans prefer black women over their own species—did little to hide its bluntness. Confronted with "that immoveable veil of black which covers all the emotions of the other race," Jefferson retreated to the safety—behind the further veil—of primitive, infantile fantasy.

There may be no reason now to take Jefferson too much to task—and there would have been less reason, say, in 1940, the year Richard Wright's *Native Son* exploded into the American imagination, releasing the Jim Crow nightmare in splendid horror. Described by the press in the novel as an "ape," a "missing link in the human species," a "jungle beast . . . in the grip of a brain-numbing sex passion," Bigger Thomas is the paradoxical cry of oppression and its violent protest, of fantastic fear and its requited realization. His "rape" and murder of Mary Dalton is terrible precisely because of the double pressure of fate and coincidence that brings it about; but in the press it is ascribed to the "minor portion of white blood in his veins, a mixture which generally makes for a criminal and intractable nature." Exposing the brutal rebellion a misconceived liberalism can produce, *Native Son* nonetheless transcends the actual violence it depicts in the hallucination of protest that, like a mirroring image, like the mask of a mask, pervades and creates the character of Bigger: "He wished that he could be an ideal in their minds; that his black face and the image of his smothering Mary and cutting off her head and burning her could hover before their eyes as a terrible picture of reality which they could see and feel and yet not destroy." The prosecution's assertion that Bigger burns Mary's body in order "to destroy evidence of offenses *worse* than rape," to obliterate the "marks of his teeth . . . on the innocent white flesh of her breasts," reminiscent as it is of *The Clansman,* is unnervingly countered by the greater, more legitimate violence in Bigger's own mind: "He committed rape every time he looked into a white face. He was a long, taut piece of rubber which a thousand white hands had stretched to the snapping point, and when he snapped it was rape. But it was [also] rape when he cried out in hate deep in his heart as he felt the strain of living day by day."

Had it been Jefferson, Mississippi, rather than Chicago, Bigger would perhaps not, as the prosecutor goes on to remark, "have been accorded the high honor of sitting here in this court of law!" and of being executed by the machinery of deliberate justice. The difference between Joe Christmas and Bigger Thomas as deliberate, even stylized symbols of requisite sacrifice should not be ignored; but the enslaving fate that surrounds each of them, expressing a thorough interpenetration of fantasy and reality, is as similar as the details of their crimes— similar to the point that Bigger, in what seems a deliberate echo of Faulkner's refrain concerning the fate of Christmas, says early on, "Sometimes I feel like something awful's going to happen to me." Of course everything that happens to Bigger and to Joe Christmas is awful. But whereas Wright's risk lay in the lure of a Marxist ideology that threatens to flatten out Bigger's tragedy, the risk in the case of Faulkner's novel is that the awful, forced to extremity in the grandiose rhythms of the prose and in the relentless probing of depravity, will become comic. Indeed, *Light in August* often verges on the burlesque horror of *Sanctuary,* but only at two points—in its delineation of Joanna Burden's murder and in Percy Grimm's bicycle chase of Christmas—does it slip over the edge, at both points in recoil from the greatest acts of violence the novel contains. The second, because it leads to the slaughter of Christmas, has the greater significance as an ironic, anticipatory release of pressure; the first, however, increases in splendor for having come straight out of Faulkner's Southern precursor, Poe.

The passerby who discovers the fire and then the nearly decapitated body of Joanna Burden is afraid "to pick her up and carry her out because her head might come clean off." Her throat slashed ear to ear, Joanna seemed an intentional mirror image of Madame L'Espanaye, who in "The Murders in the Rue Morgue" (1841) is decapitated by an orangutan wielding his master's razor. When her corpse is picked up, the head falls off. Insofar as Poe's story should be read in part as an oblique, libidinous racial fantasy, the details of the murder, the fear of whipping that initiates it, and the focus on the beast's mimic shaving with his murder weapon all have their relevant analogues in *Light in August.* Faulkner does not bring the razor into such powerful symbolic focus as Melville had in *Benito Cereno,* and nowhere in *Light in August* does he directly compare Joe Christmas to an orangutan: he did not have to, so much was the "Negro as beast" a part of Southern— and American—racial iconography. And though we should note as well that he was probably drawing on a similar murder of a white woman by decapitation with a razor (followed by the lynching and castration of the black murderer) that occurred near Oxford in 1908, it is the heritage of racial violence, surrounding this actual murder as well as its fictional counterpart and enveloping both in the convulsive fantasies of blood violation, that must be seen to contain *within* it the power of *Light in August*. As Christmas himself both contains, and is contained within, a myth, so the novel embodies within itself the many threads of racial myth—unwinding and rewinding in both Faulkner's career and his nation's history—that in a larger way embodies it.

The murder of Joanna Burden, which appears as a kind of shadow play of weapons, revolver and razor, and which follows from her final attempt to get Christmas to kneel with her in prayer, is the last, antagonistic expression of the violence their combative sexual affair has mimicked all along. As such it casts back to the ritual sacrifice Joe performs to cleanse himself of the horror of menstrual blood ("It's something that happens to them once a month," his companion had said) and forecasts the ambiguous absolution he finds kneeling behind a table when he is murdered in Hightower's house. Enveloping the two murders and the affair that produces them, and enveloping the novel and the heritage that produces it, is the potent symbol of "the black shadow in the shape of a cross" that Joanna invokes at the climax of her family's story. Although the shadowed cross is black, the crucified are white; the "shadow in which" all live, black and white, is the perfectly ambiguous expression of the burden of white *within* black *within* white—of what her father calls "a race doomed and cursed to be forever and ever a part of the white race's doom and curse for its sins." There is no need to go through the contortions some readers have to see Christmas as a Christ figure; his career simply includes that potential significance (as, in a different fashion, Lincoln's career did) but surpasses any actual relevance it could have—except (here again like Lincoln) as the ironically tortured emblem that releases into the surging rhythms of racial fantasy the degeneration of Southern gynealotry (Joanna Burden), the tautological frenzy of zealous racism (Doc Hines), the last gasp of the Lost Cause (Hightower), and the dream come true of the Invisible Empire (Percy Grimm). What it does more conclusively is continue to depict the psychological confusion in (and quite nearly the inversion of) the relationship between master and slave, in which a literal and visible ascendancy is engulfed by one that is figurative and invisible. Joe Christmas lives between these two possibilities, passes between them, and it is there that he dies.

Faulkner began *Light in August* in August of 1931, the centennial anniversary of Nat Turner's bloody rebellion in Southampton, Virginia. The Turner insurrection, in which some fifty whites were murdered, erupted out of nowhere—or so it seemed to many Southerners. A religious fanatic who early in his life had apocalyptic visions of "white spirits and black spirits engaged in battle," of lighted figures in the sky stretched "from east to west, even as they were extended on the cross on Calvary for the redemption of sinners," Turner claimed in the purported confessions recorded by Thomas Gray that he was divinely inspired to take up Christ's yoke and "fight against the Serpent, for the time was fast approaching when the first should be last and the last should be first." The threat of Turner's rebellion was thus mitigated in some minds by his madness; only insanity could lead otherwise contented slaves to such brutal atrocities. Aside from the crazed rebel slave in Harriet Beecher Stowe's *Dred* (1856), Turner received little significant literary attention until the appearance in 1967 of William Styron's *The Confessions of Nat Turner,* a novel designed to reassure no one, black or white.

The aspect of Styron's searing fictional account of Turner's life that has aroused most controversy is his explicit portrayal of Turner's imagined sexual attraction to several white women, most particularly to the white girl who appears to be the only person Turner himself actually killed. If this part of the novel is to be deprecated, however, it must also be measured, for example, against the portrayal of "rape" in *Native Son.* Turner's desire (as Styron depicts it) to fill his future victim with "warm milky spurts of desecration" or, in another instance, to repay the "pity" and "compassion" of a weak white woman with "outrageous spurts of defilement" and produce in her "the swift and violent immediacy of a pain of which I was complete overseer," is nothing less than the actualization of a fantasy that may have existed during slavery (although Turner's insurrection, among others, was remarkably free from such sexual retribution) but arose more clearly in the twentieth century *between* black and white, making deceptively confused the masks that faced and reflected each other, and enclosing both in the violence the threat of amalgamation could release. Without minimizing the important differences between the situations and the historical renderings of Bigger Thomas and Styron's Nat Turner, we should note as well that from the standpoint of their creators they are two sides of a coin, two masks of violence turning against itself in redoubled, nearly tautological frenzy. The power driving this frenzy, as James Baldwin has observed in the case of Bigger, is simply that of a "complementary faith among the damned," which may lead them at last to a forcing "into the arena of the actual those fantastic crimes of which they have been accused, achieving their vengeance and their own destruction through making the nightmare real" (*Notes of a Native Son*).

Faulkner was dead by the time Styron's novel appeared; he thought well of *Native Son;* and there is no evidence, aside from the coincidence of the date he began *Light in August,* that he knew or cared much about Nat Turner. But the psychology of amalgamation, and the violence it responds to and extends, are rendered visible on nearly every page of Faulkner's novel. It is a psychology that thoroughly depends on the paradox of retributive violence—a paradox Faulkner often described in response to questions about violence in his fiction as something "man must combat" even when "he has been strangled by degradation and violence, when he has hated the violence he participated in, when he has resisted the violence, when he believed in something like honor and pride and compassion, even in degradation" (Meriwether and Millgate, eds.). Sex, he added, has much the same function; indeed, it is difficult to conceive of their separation in his novels, so completely do they penetrate each other, like white and black. Because violence and sexuality determine the contours of the South's romance of blood, it is worth pointing out again that the relationship between *Sanctuary* and *Light in August,* Faulkner's two most violent and sexual novels, is an important one. As we noted earlier, the ambiguous delineation of Popeye as a "black man" casts back in the American tradition toward Hawthorne's probing of the secret thrills of Puritan repression, and at the same time prefigures Faulkner's confrontation in *Light in August, Absalom, Absalom!,* and *Go Down, Moses* of the more haunting, more historically immediate complexity of that repression. By making literal in Joe Christmas the figurative coloring of Popeye and extending by a single degree the nymphomania of Temple Drake into the comic depravity of Joanna Burden, Faulkner himself passed the color line that would define his major work and extend the boundaries of classic American fiction to include a tormenting problem that underlay each successive challenge to the failing vision of democratic freedom.

Faulkner's struggle with the problem of narrative form up to and including *Light in August* must therefore be seen to contain as well his evolving effort to include a tradition that is both larger than his own and yet in the twentieth century completely dependent on it. *Light in*

August, heaving and bulging with the effort to integrate those traditions, barely survives the pressure it produces, but it turns Faulkner, as it would Styron, back toward the century in which the amalgamation of America and the South seemed least likely and became most crucial. The accounts of those readers of *Light in August* who have tried to emphasize that Christmas is characteristic of the "isolated, doomed heroes" of classic American fiction; that he takes his place in the "descending spiral of isolation, rebellion, and denial" that is "the heritage of American negation"; or that he personifies "the most extreme phase conceivable of American loneliness," are thus correct but require a different emphasis. The critics I quote from here [Richard Chase, Maxwell Geismar, Alfred Kazin] hardly deny the importance of race, but they focus on a problem of literary characterization that in the case of *Light in August* both contains, and must be subordinated to, a more particular social one. "The problem of the twentieth century," W. E. B. Du Bois remarked in *The Souls of Black Folk* (1903), "is the problem of the color-line." By embodying that problem in a character whose very physical and emotional self embodies the sexual violence of racial conflict, Faulkner made the problem painfully visible and immediate.

He did so most evidently by enacting in the novel's form the crisis that motivates its action. We have already noted that Christmas both dominates the novel and threatens to tear it apart, and that the peculiar form of the novel derives in large part from the way in which the characters of Joanna Burden, Hines, Hightower, and Grimm come into being in the long plunges into the past that contact with Christmas brings about. The actualization of their lives, in bold, alienating movements away from a line of integrated narrative action, expresses in the novel's form a crisis responding to the violent crisis of blood that the contagion of Christmas represents. Donald Kartiganer is thus right to say that, because the novel's isolated characters and scenes all "revolve around, and blur into, [the] impenetrable center" of Christmas's story, even as the story itself "dissolves into expanding configurations of meaning," *Light in August* is a novel whose form "feeds on its own dissolution." What is most striking about the novel is that despite the later novel's extraordinary increase in narrative and syntactical complexity *Light in August* is much harder to keep in focus than *Absalom, Absalom!* The radical involution of fiction within fiction in the story of Charles Bon has no equal moment in *Light in August,* in which the crisis of blood, the "containing" of black within white,

white within black, derives its power from collision, penetration, and withdrawal rather than from the dramatic marriages of opposing forces that Faulkner would strive for in Quentin's and Shreve's imaginative reconstructions. Both the action and the form of *Light in August* answer violence with violence, tearing away from each other lives and stories as they threaten to become joined. At a psychological level they do indeed blur into each other; but at a narrative level that responds to the deepest need of that psychology, they remain vivid and powerless in their segregation.

It is for good reason, then, that in accounting for Christmas's flight to Hightower's house Faulkner first raises the possibility of "like to like" and then replaces it with Gavin Stevens's equally inadequate theory of a battle in Christmas between white blood and black blood. The long, most isolating plunge into the past of Hightower that follows Christmas's death offers little that is relevant to Christmas's life, or even to Hightower's act of providing him with a futile, last-minute alibi—little, that is, but one of the many tortured myths that lie behind the enslavement in which Joe Christmas, like Jim Crow, is still trapped. Christmas's act of striking down Hightower, like a "vengeful and furious god pronouncing doom," issues only in the overcharged, overcompensating rhetoric of Hightower's final visions of the haloed wheel and the tumultuous rush of cavalry. As though spending in wild abandon the accumulated fury he could not bring into the focus of dramatic involvement, Faulkner tears away from each other the two characters who might most conceivably have been linked. They remain connected only by the slender threads of Faulkner's recurring plot of skipped generations, tied and untied with merciless haste, and by the fanatical exclamations of abomination and bitchery that mercilessly isolate Christmas's grandfather. Both the sexual frenzy of Hines and the visions of Hightower that are its ironic, sublimated correlary are surpassed in significance by the act of sacrifice that the one leads toward and the other falls away from. The "single instant of darkness" in which each of them continues to live can neither approach nor further elaborate the visionary scene of Christmas's death that grows out of Percy Grimm's violent act and his swift, brutal proclamation:

> "Now you'll let white women alone, even in hell," he said.
> But the man on the floor had not moved. He just lay there,
> with his eyes open and empty of everything save conscious-
> ness, and with something, a shadow about his mouth. For a

long moment he looked up at them with peaceful and unfathomable and unbearable eyes. Then his face, body, all, seemed to collapse, to fall in upon itself, and from out of the slashed garments about his hips and loins the pent black blood seemed to rush like a released breath. It seemed to rush out of his pale body like the rush of sparks from a rising rocket; upon the black blast the man seemed to rise soaring into their memories forever and ever.

Christmas's passive, suicidal participation in this act is one of several features that have led readers to envision him as a Christ figure. When he was once asked about this, Faulkner simply replied that because there are, after all, very few plots in the world of literature and because "that Christ story is one of the best" that has been "invented," it is likely that "it will recur." When Christmas rises "forever and ever" into the memories of his executioners, the Christ story recurs in a fragmented form that depends on it ironically at best. It certainly depends upon it less, for example, than does *Uncle Tom's Cabin* (1852), whose author quite rightly claimed to have depicted nothing "that equals the frightful reality of scenes daily and hourly acting on our shores, beneath the shadow of American law, and the shadow of the cross of Christ," but seemed also to believe that only the "sons of white fathers" among slaves, only those with the "haughty feelings" of Anglo-Saxon blood "burning in their veins," could rise in revolt "and raise with them their mother's race." Stowe, of course, meant to increase her rhetorical power by these remarks rather than undermine it. But as Baldwin has trenchantly observed of the novel whose hero acquires his superhuman powers of humiliating endurance from a vision of the suffering Christ, *Uncle Tom's Cabin* wears the secret "mask of cruelty." Although it poses as a catalogue of actual crimes and heart-rending violence, its emphatic racist sentimentalism betrays a "theological terror, the terror of damnation," which in the end is "not different from that terror which activates a lynch mob." As Baldwin's challenging remarks suggest, the terror behind Stowe's mask may be the distinguishing characteristic of a drama of repression, which when it is inverted leads directly to Bigger Thomas, who is so much Uncle Tom's contemporary descendant, "flesh of his flesh," that if the books are placed together it seems Stowe and Wright (not at all unlike Joanna Burden and Joe Christmas, we might add) "are locked together in a deadly, timeless battle; the one uttering merciless exhortations, the other shouting curses" (*Notes of a Native Son*).

To see this inversion clearly and to measure the changing climate of racial fantasy that makes it possible, we need only to place *Light in August* between the two books and their authors. Welding together the suffering passivity of Uncle Tom and the violent rage of Bigger Thomas, Joe Christmas, his own blood violently released in retribution for the blood he has spilt and violated, is surrounded on the one hand by the theological terror of Joanna Burden and Doc Hines, and on the other by its twentieth-century machinery of execution, the hysterical, overbearing violence of Percy Grimm. Christmas's death is as much a "lynching" as he is a "Negro"; that is, technical details do not count here. What counts is the fantasy Christmas embodies and exposes in others by appearing to act "like a nigger," by releasing formally and actually what Walter White called "the Frankenstein monster" of lynching, which puts its creators in fear of their own creation and threatens to bring about more violence than it can ever control. It is thus significant that Faulkner agreed with Cowley that the Percy Grimm section should be anthologized in *The Portable Faulkner;* for as Faulkner remarked at that later date, he had "created a Nazi" before Hitler did, a "Fascist galahad who saved the white race by murdering Christmas" (*Faulkner Cowley File*).

The power of the analogy between slavery and fascism, both productive of complex psychological infusions of overt hatred with infantalizing dependency, has been noted by historians and literary critics alike. We need not accept it in detail here in order to see that the sacrifice of Joe Christmas by Percy Grimm—a sacrifice made in the name of a thorough denial, not just of the threat Christmas poses, but of the one he already *contains within him* as its requisite opposite—is exceeded in actual violence by the hallucinating specter that momentarily coalesces into a physical act. The physical violence of the sacrifice, like the sexual contagion it responds to, is enveloped in a violence that knows no tactile, containing bounds. One might well speak, then, of a *form* of violence that corresponds in part to the novel's displayed struggle with the *form* of Christmas's life and story; as his very existence sets in motion, but cannot be controlled by, the fantasies it arouses, so his murder cannot in any clear or final way, can with no catharsis or resolution, control or make meaningful their pattern. In this respect, Christmas's death is utterly opposed, for example, to that of Billy Budd, which conforms in measured, stately fashion to the mechanisms of justice that create and define Captain Vere's fatherly authority and reenforce the Christology of his victim.

Christmas's death is a sacrifice not because he sees it that way, or because Percy Grimm necessarily does, or even because the novel suggests that it is; rather, it is sacrificial in that it depends on the "mechanism of reciprocal violence," which René Girard has shown to be the origin of, and to be fully expressed by, ritual sacrifice. The reciprocal violence Girard describes is a "vicious circle" from which the community, once it has entered, is unable to extricate itself without selecting a surrogate victim who can contain the spread of violence by taking it upon himself. As such, the surrogate victim may be seen as a "monstrous double," a figure who is both inside and outside the community, who embodies all its possible differences, and thus "constitutes both a link and a barrier between the community and the sacred" (*Violence and the Sacred*). In designating Christmas a surrogate victim, we should be quick to note that he is no more carefully selected to die as a way of warding off further violence than he is, in his death, able to do so. The violence continues to spread—in the lives of the novel and in Faulkner's own novels of the next twenty years; in the agony of Jim Crow that Faulkner's novels and public declarations could do little to stop; and in the fantasies of violated blood that racial equality paradoxically resists and promotes. Like the contagion of sexual violence represented in the menstrual blood that horrifies Christmas by its monstrous significance, the contagion of violence that grows out of the fear of miscegenation represents a menace that has visible actualizations but invisible meaning.

Although Faulkner apparently never witnessed a lynching, his life was surrounded by them. From at least two of them he drew the materials of *Light in August* and *Intruder in the Dust;* in the second he would temporarily resolve the crisis of blood, but in the first he gave way to the full horror it could release. Christmas is not a surrogate victim in the precise sense Girard describes, but as the "white nigger" he is very much, almost too much a monstrous double, for he contains— mask to mask, in mirroring images—the community's own projected desires and fears as well as their reciprocal realization. Like Twain's monstrous double, Tom Driscoll, who wears charcoal blackface when he murders his white "father," Joe Christmas embodies the twin acts of vengeance and sacrifice, neither of them within his control nor clearly ascribable to a conscious act of will; but unlike Tom and unlike Bigger Thomas, Melville's Babo, or Nat Turner, Joe is not "decently hung by a force, a principle" but, as his grandmother fears, is "hacked . . . dead by a Thing." That "thing" is not simply Percy Grimm (who is only its symbol, as Christmas himself is the symbolic embodiment of miscegenation) but an awesome power Faulkner can only account for by the mystic invocation of Fate—the "Player." Likewise, Christmas's castration, the mirroring affirmation and denial of sexuality, is a grotesque distortion of violent reciprocity. Occurring outside the sacrificial process of justice whose machinery may take the place of surrogate victimization in the control of contagious violence, the form of Christmas's death ensures, as White and Twain observed of lynching, that such violence will go on. The legitimized, legal violence with which *Native Son, Pudd'nhead Wilson, Benito Cereno,* and Nat Turner's rebellion all end serves to remind us that the shocking violence of *Light in August* depends in large part on its vitiating and overwhelming a system that cannot control it. As Faulkner put it quite appropriately in an episode that is otherwise humorous (the useless bloodhounds employed to track Christmas): "It was as if the very initial outrage of the murder carried in its wake and made of all subsequent actions something monstrous and paradoxical and wrong, in themselves against both reason and nature."

This loss of control, this monstrous swelling of paradoxical actions is expressed, again, not just in the blasphemous character of Christmas himself, but also in the novel's form from beginning to end—most particularly, of course, from the moment the murder of Joanna Burden begins a third of the way into the novel. It is precisely at that point that the nearly uncontrollable fury of Faulkner's narrative is released. The threat of physical amalgamation, of the disintegration of racial distinctions, erupts into a violent assertion of distinctions— one that radically denies the physical amalgamation that already exists and the psychological amalgamation that follows from it; and one that leads Faulkner, in the face of such a blurring of emotions, to an equally violent and alienating narrative form. The attempt to unite the crisis of blood and the crisis of narrative form continues beyond *Light in August* in the more precisely probed and controlled violence of *Absalom, Absalom!* and *Go Down, Moses,* and it may be said to continue in the consciously measured and carefully worded rhythms of Faulkner's later public statements on the question of race. Like Twain's "imitation nigger," no less the "monstrous freak" than the Siamese twins his character grew from, and like Twain himself, Faulkner was haunted by an unanswerable question: "Why were niggers *and* whites made? What crime did the uncreated first nigger commit that the curse of birth was decreed for him? And why this awful difference made between white and black?" *Light in August* begins Faulkner's stunning explorations of that question, explorations that would lead him deeper into his own past and into the past of his own first fiction; deeper into a history that came more visibly and paradoxically into focus as his career became more public and his native country more stridently recalcitrant on the question of race; and deeper into a moral and psychological problem that engulfs the promise of freedom. It would lead him next to an epic rendering of his country's epic trauma: the trauma of the house divided.

Figures of Division: *Light in August*

James A. Snead

Faulkner, faced with the problematics of racial division and himself seeking figures of merging and synthesis, presents in *Light in August* a man both masculine and feminine, both black and white, a "tragic mulatto," an American double-being who breaks all the semiotic codes of society. In his novels of his mid-thirties, Faulkner seems to be working out the question whether such a reconciliatory, almost mythical figure might transcend in fiction the dire antagonisms of life. In the already "conventional" anti-traditionalism of the modern era, we have seen that vision begins with figures of merging: "The attraction of reconciliation is the elective breeding-ground of false models and metaphors" (Paul de Man, *Allegories of Reading*). But it must be added that "false models and metaphors" are also the feeding-ground of most great writing. In more traditional Western thought, merging is considered a chaotic condition which threatens the structures of society, language, and identity. Joe Christmas, Charles Bon, and Lucas Beauchamp (the central figures of *Light in August, Absalom, Absalom!,* and *Go Down, Moses*—all mulattoes), far from being ideal solutions to racial polarity, come to seem exactly those points of chaos that threaten to destroy every plot of false serenity. Insofar as Joe Christmas and Charles Bon cannot signify any one thing, they must finally undercut the very possibility of unitary significance. The tragic realization of these novels may be that a kind of semiotic discrimination is as

From *Figures of Division: William Faulkner's Major Novels.* © 1986 by James A. Snead. Methuen & Co., 1986.

necessary to reading as it is, deplorably, for the whites of Jefferson, Mississippi.

Having depicted and arrived at this brink, Faulkner—no less than Jefferson—shows a conservative compulsion to impose order. In the killings of Joe Christmas and Charles Bon, society represses by violence the proofs of its own brokenness, yet cannot erase the double debris—both of its initial collapse and of its violent repressions. In other words, the post-modernist reconciliation in Faulkner culminates precisely in the destruction of that which had seemed to remedy modernism's atomizations. Yet this destruction cannot but seem a restoration of the past and as such not a promising Second Coming, but rather a very weary déjà vu. *Light in August* presents a cyclical movement: the town goes from certainty about what race signifies and what signifies race, through an experience that disrupts that surety, and back again to a forced reestablishment of certainty. Christmas and Bon give the promise of reconcilement, but also remind of an original, violent, sundering. Therefore they must be eliminated. But to murder them does not restore a unified past; it simply repeats a former separation by force.

What the Town Knows

Consensus arises in the performative mode. The early pages of *Light in August* overflow with tropes of domination in the town's common parlance: "Starting in at daylight and slaving all day like a durn nigger"; "Well, maybe some folks work like the niggers work where they come from." Lucas Burch repeats this simile later on, referring to himself: "Slaving like a durn nigger ten hours a day." This trope would engrave in language by repetition the economic connection between blacks and "slaving"—a class rigidification that has ensured the economic stability of Jefferson and, more generally, American society. Hearsay would virtually write behavior, making it inflexible in the reality of these commonplaces. Byron Bunch says of Joanna Burden: "they say she is still mixed up with niggers. . . . Folks say she claims that niggers are the same as white folks." What "they say" may be true or false, but because "they say it" it seems the truth.

We have seen just a few examples of significant reference points in Jefferson language. A black is a certain thing; a black does certain jobs. To find these rhetorics in well-socialized speakers is one thing, but it is quite another to find them in the voice of the narrator. Faulkner gives us the choice to be racists in a very cunning way: do we passively accept the truth of the narrator's judgment and thereby ourselves join the town's consensus? Or do we suspend our own judgment for the sake of fairness? There is, for instance, the text's repeated notion that blacks smell different from whites: "before he knew it he was in Freedman Town, surrounded by the summer smell . . . of invisible negroes"; "He could smell Negro"; "the same children, with different names; the same grown people, with different smells." Outrageously the narrator wants bodily odor here to replace the visual signifier of race that Joe Christmas has now made defunct (dark skin color), but his subterfuge is transparent. Umberto Eco includes *olfactory signs* among the possible components of a general cultural semiotics, citing Baudelaire's notion of a "code of scents," or Peirce's notion of smell as an "index"—hence olfactory signals are as apt to be abused by socio-economic "marking" (presumably, they designated a "natural" difference) as any other sort (*A Theory of Semiotics*).

Earlier, we have read the following sentences:

> He [Armstid] got into the wagon and waked the mules. That is, he put them into motion, since *only a negro can tell when a mule is asleep or awake.*

> None of them knew then where Christmas lived and what he was actually doing *behind the veil, the screen, of his negro's job at the mill* . . . even the ones who bought the whiskey did not know that Christmas was actually living in *a tumble down negro cabin* on Miss Burden's place, and that he had been living in it for more than two years.

> Hightower knew that the man would walk all the way to town and then spend probably thirty minutes more getting in touch with a doctor, *in his fumbling and timeless negro fashion,* instead of asking some white woman to telephone for him. (My italics)

The italicized statements demonstrate a highly revealing yet suspect alternation of ignorance and knowledge. The first shows that "a negro" knows whether a mule is awake or asleep—no doubt because of a connection "they say" exists between blacks and the natural world of animals. In the second, "everyone" ostensibly knows what a "negro cabin" is: the kind of cabin where a Negro would live. But here the narrator even seems to know more than "they" do. He sees "behind the veil" of a job that "everyone knows" would ordinarily be a "negro's." In the third example Hightower knows the future behavior of blacks already, as if sequence were reversed, and future action had preceded the present. But these statements, which seem absolutely correct versions of reality, are quite duplicitous. For example, if "only a negro" can really know a mule, then the Negro knows more than both the white narrator and Hightower. In the second example, the narrator does not simply say "job at the mill" but "negro's job at the mill." Joe Christmas hides his "blackness" behind the screen of a "negro's job": he pretends to "slave like a negro" so no one will think he is one. But the very category of "Negro" ("negro's job . . . negro cabin") may be seen as a screen, a veil of only apparent difference that society may be using to disguise actual similarities. Therefore, the narrator has yet to see through "Negro," even though he has seen through the "job." Possibly the whole white society, like the "white" Christmas, is hiding behind the veil of "Negro" (recall Quentin's "a nigger is . . . a form of behaviour; a sort of obverse reflection of the white people he lives among"). One citizen says, "That nigger murderer. Christmas," but says in the next breath, "He dont look no more like a nigger than I do, either." Finally, Hightower, in the third example, predicts that any black will "naturally" hesitate under certain circumstances. Yet he selectively omits to mention that such hesitation comes from the standard consequence—lynching and castration—of a black male "asking some white woman" anything, even "to telephone for him": "Now you'll let white women alone, even in hell," Grimm says over Christmas's emasculated corpse, "flinging behind him the bloody butcher knife." Hightower, typically for Yoknapatawpha, represses society's threats and acts of violence, while highlighting what are blacks' "natural" and "timeless" "fashions." He shows a willed ignorance (akin to Freudian dream censorship) that must ultimately condition all questions of knowledge and ignorance in the novel.

Light in August, Absalom, Absalom!, and *Go Down, Moses* treat, more informatively than their predecessors, the relationship between language and knowledge. At question is, above all, what the town knows, what it thinks it knows, what it knows but must conceal, and finally what it can never know because the knowledge would imperil its ability to know anything. In *Light in August* Faulkner diverges from Fielding's omniscient narrators or Conrad's and James's unreliable ones by exposing omniscience as unreliability. The unreliability is an active deception. There is no deficiency, of either intelligence or perspicacity:

the narrator is actively creating error. Society here turns arbitrary codes of dominance into "fact." To make matters worse, the reader helps accomplish the entire process.

The narrator wishes to surpass in accuracy a malleable "oral" account, claiming to know what others do not. Oral tales are flexible, subject to skepticism: Lena says, "most of what folks tells on other folks ain't true to begin with." The novel is quite knowledgeable about lack of knowledge in others: "it is possible that she did not know this at the time"; "they did not know who he was . . . none of them had the sense to recognise it"; "they still do not know for certain if Christmas is connected with it . . . some of them know that Christmas and Brown both live in a cabin." Oral accounts strive—as written narrative does—for rigidity and invariance leading to credibility. "They say" always yearns to become "it is written." The written always vaunts authority over the told, which it must place within quotations marks.

HABIT AND MISRECOGNITION

Reading and gossip seem to offer something new to be told, but both operations essentially involve recognizing the old in the new, hence misrecognizing what one sees. *Light in August,* despite its "emphasis on perception," is actually about what people fail to perceive. Most often, characters remain ignorant either because they cannot look, or because they think they do "not need to look to know." The assumption that omniscience is a real prediction of the future turns out badly. Christmas represents the aporia that comes when real events do not replicate social expectations. All the ways of custom and habit are blocked or at best circular.

Perception seems particularly difficult between races and sexes. Martha and her husband Armstid, for example, seem in different worlds:

> He does not look in that direction; he does not need to look
> to know that she will be there, is there. . . . He does not
> watch her. . . . He does not need to. . . . He does not look
> at her. . . . He begins to wash, his back to her. . . . Mrs
> Armstid does not look around. . . . And he can feel her
> looking at him. . . . He cannot tell from her voice if she is
> watching him or not now. . . . And now he knows that she
> is watching him.

Habituation (akin in this context to an optical effect: persistence of vision) tends to obscure whatever it fixes. Lena and her male driver never look at each other; each knows what the other "is": "Apparently he has never looked at her. . . . Apparently she has never looked at him, either. She does not do so now." Byron and Burch mirror each other when they speak, called "the one" and "the other": "Byron thinks that this is just the reflection of what he himself already knows and is about to tell. . . . He is not looking at the other now." At times, distraction is the culprit. When the young couple stop their car for him, Christmas does not actually register their words: "Christmas did not notice this at the time. . . . Christmas did not hear this either. . . . But again Christmas did not notice . . . he was not even paying attention."

Misrecognition, whether caused by oversight or self-delusion, is the central theme in *Light in August,* and the novel shares this concern with *Don Quixote,* which Faulkner invariably listed among those books that had influenced him most. Readers misperceive before anyone else, as at the beginning of chapter 2: "the group of men at work in the planer shed looked up, and saw the stranger standing there, watching them." Our immediate temptation is to think that "the stranger" is Lucas Burch, whom Lena Grove has been seeking in chapter 1. But "the stranger" is Christmas, whom we meet here, unnamed, for the first time. Christmas himself misperceives crucial moments in his life, such as when the dietitian offers him "hush money": "When he saw the hand emerge from the pocket he believed that she was about to strike him. But she did not; the hand just opened beneath his eyes. Upon it lay a silver dollar." Joe seems generally unable to understand the visible and audible signs of society: his mother puts "into the can beneath his round grave eyes coins whose value he did not even recognise." Christmas misunderstands Max and Mame: "it was as if they talked at and because of him, in a language which he did not understand"; "Perhaps he heard the words. But likely not. Likely they were as yet no more significant than the rasping of insects beyond the closedrawn window, or the packed bags which he had looked at and had not yet seen."

Joe Christmas's ignorance is also a kind of sexual innocence. As a boy, his older friends know about sex. The younger ones, Christmas included, "did not know that. They did not know that all girls wanted to, let alone that there were times when they could not." He misunderstands the name "Bobbie," calling it "A man's name." Bobbie

Allen has two men's names, and as a result helps create Joe's general confusion about gender. Forgetting what he had learned about menstruation, Joe listens to Bobbie saying to him that she cannot go to bed with him: " 'Listen. I'm sick tonight.' He did not understand. He said nothing. Perhaps he did not need to understand." Bobbie Allen is also a prostitute, but Joe does not seem to understand:

> "I thought you knew," she said.
> "No," he said. "I reckon I didn't."
> "I thought you did."
> "No," he said. "I dont reckon I did."

Joe wrongly thinks that Max and Mame reject him because of his sexual designs on Bobbie Allen: "Very likely until the last he still believed that Max and Mame had to be placated, not for the actual fact, but because of his presence there." But Joe has misread the telltale signs of prostitution; he cannot read the language: " 'I dont even know what they are saying to her,' he thought, thinking *I dont even know that what they are saying to her is something that men do not say to a passing child.*"

SIGNIFYING "X"MAS

Joe finds the world puzzling, but the world in turn finds him indecipherable. *Light in August* depicts how Joe Christmas resists signification, while showing that we cannot tolerate anything that does not signify. Like Jefferson, readers seem compelled to supply anything that makes Christmas significant, even what is not in the text. It is as revealing as it is embarrassing to consider how many readers fall into the same racist mentality as Jefferson, even despite Faulkner's own admonition that Christmas "himself didn't know who he was—didn't know whether he was part Negro or not and would never know." Early critics, especially, insisted on calling Christmas a "harried mulatto" or a "white Negro." Some credited Gavin Stevens's intentionally ludicrous "blood" theory, discussing "a sinister figure haunted by knowledge of his negro blood." Others described "the conflict in Christmas of the white and the negro blood." Cleanth Brooks is correct to say "we are never given any firm proof that Joe Christmas possesses Negro blood"—indeed, at one point Joanna asks Joe how he knows one of his parents is "part nigger." Joe answers, "I don't know it." The simple basis of "not knowing" about Joe's race (onto which others project would-be knowledge) is the chief rhetorical prerequisite for interpreting the novel. The novel poses a challenge to our own self-reading: do we comply with or resist the signification of Joe Christmas as "nigger"?

Throughout the novel, Christmas is the sign of resistance to fixed signs. He is the quintessence of indeterminable essence. He is ambiguous from his first description: "the stranger . . . looked like a tramp, yet not like a tramp either." We never actually discover his true age. Even his name can be written "Christmas" or "Xmas" (and is, within three lines). He symbolizes the frustration and resistance that knowledge encounters whenever it wants to become permanent, or "written." In the context of the town, he is above all a matter of "rumor," and the chief episodes involving his flight and capture come to us as oral conjecture or "telling." Conjecture and oral narration are key modes here because so much knowledge in Jefferson is partial. Consequently, we immediately assimilate the town's hearsay narrative. One might even suggest that the town wishes to capture and confine Joe's meaning more than his actual body.

Critical conjecture about the meaning of the Joe Christmas figure and its containing narrative attests to this wish. The reception of Joe Christmas by the town resembles the reception of the novel by the critical community, whose general perplexity revolves around the problem of "unity of plot." The "unity" problem has close ties with the "abstraction" issue, about which there is considerable disagreement. One critic can say that Joe Christmas is an idea rather than a person, a character who "remains almost completely opaque," while another claims that "Christmas seems immediately and indisputably real."

Bobbie Allen watches Joe leave her sight, and misperceives what she seems to see: "As he faded on down the road, the shape, the shadow, she believed that he was running. . . . He was not running." He is an elusive shadow. Writing is Faulkner's metaphor here, and Joe Christmas avidly resists the properties and effects of written imprintation. He escapes the purview of his father McEachern by climbing down a rope "with the shadowlike agility of a cat . . . passing swift as a shadow across the window." Later "Joe, descending on his rope, slid like a fast shadow across the open and moonfilled window. . . . McEachern did not at once recognise him or perhaps believe what he saw." McEachern has just been trying, upon pain of whipping, to get Christmas to "take the book"—or learn by heart excerpts from "an enormous Bible" and "a Presbyterian catechism." Rote memorization uses Pavlovian conditioning by repetition in order to "imprint" the written text upon the mind. It is no wonder, then, that McEachern's voice "was just cold, implacable, like written or printed words." He manifests a Protestant literalism that must, upon pain of death, see the world in black and white terms.

Joe is the uncertainty that resists being made into writing. He is more an absence than anything else. From childhood, he has willed insufficiency: "Once he had owned garments with intact buttons. A woman had sewed them on. . . . With his pocket knife . . . he would cut off the buttons which she had just replaced." A woman completing the "intact buttons" of his garment also stands for the marital bond and its social sanction. If "postponement" of gratification and fear of punishment are the controlling tenets of civilization, then Joe counters them by rejecting all deferments—particularly of punishment, hating the kindness of his mother who "would try to get herself between him and the punishment," a mediation of pain that "must give it an odor, an attenuation, and aftertaste." He had exempted himself from the prolongation of touch that extends the memory of suffering.

Joe's social exclusion typically becomes a sexual alienation from which his difficulties with women may derive. While most commentators agree that Lena is a kind of "good anima" or "fertility figure" or "earth mother," few have been able to explain her place in a novel with Joe Christmas, whose "chief problem was not nearly so much his black blood or repressive upbringing as that world of women." Brooks even goes so far as to describe Christmas's "distaste for women" and "antifeminine attitude" as "a latent tendency" towards homosexuality. It seems clear, however, that, rather than seeing Lena as the "integrity and wholeness by which the alienated characters are to be judged" and opposing this "integrity" to Joe's "latent tendency," both Joe and Lena must be seen as responses to the society from which they spring. In other words, Lena's final triumph over conventions of male-female relationships is just a happier way of dealing with the same problems that Christmas fails to solve.

Joe resists writing, but he must be written. He cannot be a total absence. He dislikes traces, but he leaves them everywhere. The posse are chasing a "shadow," but an imperfect one: "They could even see the prints of his knees and hands where he had knelt to drink from a spring." In a society in which everyone is part of a "social text," socialization paradoxically means to become as white as paper. This fact applies most of all, ironically, to the blacks. The black is a shadow, and Joe is another version of what the white mind thinks a dark mystery. Blacks leave a "mark" or "trace," be it color or smell, even despite society's efforts to erase them altogether, to make their blackness a signifier of what Ellison in *Invisible Man* calls a social "invisibility." Joe senses that he is like blacks as he walks among them:

> In the wide, empty, shadow-brooded street he looked like a phantom . . . before he knew it he was in Freedman town, *surrounded by the summer smell and the summer voices of invisible negroes. They seemed to enclose him* like bodiless voices murmuring, talking, laughing, in a language not his. . . . About him the cabins were shaped blackly out of the blackness. . . . *On all sides, even within him, the bodiless fecundmellow voices* of negro women murmured. (My italics)

The effaced black is meant to be the background for society's "writing" —like a carrier wave that you are not supposed to sense, the essential yet unperceived thing that carries the "message." Hence Christmas's flesh is "a level dead parchment color," especially in the scenes where McEachern's voice, "like written or printed words," tries to get him to repeat a catechism. Yet Joe rejects being inscribed until the very end. Late in the novel the fugitive can still leave behind, "wedged into a split plank on the side of the church, a scrap of paper." This "pencilled message" is "raggedly written, as though by an unpractised hand or perhaps in the dark. . . . It was addressed to the sheriff by name and it was unprintable—a single phrase—and it was unsigned": the last white scrap of Joe's black defiance is still "unprintable" and "unsigned."

As Christmas becomes more "Negro," he becomes less vague, less "parchment-colored." Society flattens him into a backcloth that must become one or the other color:

> He watched his body grow white out of the darkness like a kodak print emerging from the liquid.

> Vanishing as he ran, vanishing upward from the head down as if he were running headfirst and laughing into something that was obliterating him like a picture in chalk being erased from a blackboard.

> The black abyss . . . into which now and at last he had actually entered, bearing now upon his ankles the definite and ineradicable gauge of its upward moving.

The townspeople accept Burch's claim that Christmas is a "nigger" mainly because it explains the inexplicable. But the narrator, while sharing this fiction, often needs to call Joe "white": "Sometimes the notes would tell him not to come until a certain hour, to that house which no white person save himself had entered in years"; "Then they saw that the man was white. . . . Then they saw that his face was not black." The vacillation between white and black in the "kodak print" and "blackboard" similes is like the confusion in the last example about whether "not black" always means white, or even whether white always means "white." The final misrecognition must be that the "dark complected" Lucas Burch most likely has a darker skin than Christmas, whom he betrays as a "nigger."

Burch, a criminally and blatantly distorted character, supplies the town with a sense of coherence by introducing at the right time divisive racial classifications. Dividing Joe Christmas from white folks immediately solves the town's problems. He restores the town's sense of identity and thereby escapes his own quandary by intensifying Joe's. Like the falsely knowledgeable narrator, Burch pretends to assert his own superior knowledge against the town's stupidity:

> "You're so smart," he says. "The folks in this town is so smart. Fooled for three years. Calling him a foreigner for three years, when soon as I watched him three days I knew he wasn't no more a foreigner than I am. . . . He's got nigger blood in him. I knowed it when I first saw him. . . . One time he even admitted it, told me he was part nigger."
>
> "A nigger," the marshal said. "I always thought there was something funny about that fellow."
>
> "Well," the sheriff says, "I believe you are telling the truth at last."

Lucas Burch is Christmas's darker double. He looks more like a "foreigner" and "nigger " and "murderer" than Christmas does (he has a "little white scar by his mouth"), and yet Christmas is the "nigger" whom the community sacrifices. In fact, by the time the lynch mob is aroused, actual color makes no difference: the "countrymen . . . believed aloud that it was an anonymous crime committed not by a negro but by Negro and [they] knew, believed, and hoped that she had been ravished too: at least once before her throat was cut and at least once afterward." The intentional humor of this excerpt is matched only by its absolute horror. Given that Joe and Lucas are really each other's "dark doubles," sharing every duty and function, it must follow that the "dark complected" Lucas, and not Joe Christmas, is likely to have "black blood." This assumption would explain why he is so anxious to "darken" and destroy Joe. Lena Grove's child, fathered by Burch, will be another mulatto in a long string of uncertain progeny that here, as in *Absalom, Absalom!*, ravels out into an uncertain future.

White Jefferson constitutes hearsay as authority, and has formed the hearsay into fixed figures to which force lends validity. For Christmas to become part of that society, he has to become one thing or an other. But he is neither/nor: neither black nor white, neither background nor writing he is, no less than Darl or Addie, socially neuter. Joe Christmas must become the object of a signifying violence. *"We'll see if his blood is black. . . . We'll need a little more blood to tell for sure,"* say the men who come to brutalize him; they certainly wish to harm Joe, but their motives are in large part definitional. Yet even their expedient of violence does not help. The more blood is spilled to distinguish black from white blood, the more difficult it is to see the difference; at a considerable price it becomes clear that black and white "blood" are the same.

The fate of Christmas demonstrates that the town signifies "natural" value by force. There is no natural way to know what Christmas is, but this is precisely what annoys the town:

> He dont look any more like a nigger than I do. But it must have been the nigger blood in him. . . . He never acted like either a nigger or a white man. That was it. That was what made the folks so mad. . . . It was like he never knew he was a murderer, let alone a nigger too.

He has not been socialized; he does not "know" what his "I" signifies. At their moment of outrage, the men of the town choose a murderous sort of coherence. In *Absalom, Absalom!* Mr Compson says of the "white Negro," Charles Etienne Bon, "he was, must be, a negro."

The moral of *Light in August*—that "when anything gets to be a habit, it also manages to get a right good distance away from truth and fact"—has yet another test-case: Gail Hightower. He deludes himself thoroughly, becoming the victim of his own self-delusions. By interposing himself in Christmas's place, he almost prevents the mob's ritual murder of Christmas at the end, yet he comes short. In almost the same sense as Christmas, he is the town's scapegoat. He is marginal, living in a "small, brown, almost concealed house . . . on what used to be the main street." Faulkner makes it quite clear that someone living in a "high tower" of thought can communicate with few in the outside world. Even "the sign, carpentered neatly by himself and by himself lettered," attracts no patrons. His sign, advertising "Art Lessons / Handpainted Xmas & Anniversary Cards / Photographs Developed," has "fading letters." Hightower, like his sign, suffers from the same malaise of communication as Joe does:

> [The fading letters] were still readable, however; though, like Hightower himself, few of the townspeople needed to read them anymore. . . . So the sign which he carpentered and lettered is even less to him than it is to the town; he is no longer conscious of it as a sign, a message . . . it is just a familiar low oblong shape without any significance at all.

Gail Hightower (like Emily Grierson) wants to be "sheltered from the harsh gale of living," but it is too late for him to return to the seminary and too soon for him to die.

The town has destroyed Hightower's life in a way that almost exactly parallels its victimization of Christmas. But his relations were already corrupted by his own misrecognition of his grandfather's heroism. He "grew to manhood among phantoms, and side by side with a ghost." Faced with the unknown or indefinable nature of history, Hightower invents a repetitive ideology of the past:

> Then Sunday he would be again in the pulpit, with his wild hands and his wild rapt eager voice in which like phantoms God and salvation and the galloping horses and his dead grandfather thundered, while below him the elders sat, and the congregation, puzzled and outraged.

The public accepts his heroization of the past while remaining somewhat uncomfortable with it; they adopt the idea that his grandfather was "shot from the saddle of a galloping horse in a Jefferson street." Public opinion, however, cannot digest the idea that his wife has a lover in Memphis. Hearsay fulfills itself: "the ladies . . . maybe wondering if he knew what they believed that they already knew." "The town," "the neighbors," "the ladies," begin to construct their own version of things. They ignore Hightower's "slatternly" wife; their fictional constructs even change what they see: "And soon it was as though she were not there; that the minister did not even have a wife."

When "Sunday morning's paper" says "she had jumped or fallen from a hotel window in Memphis," it confirms the narrative that "everyone had agreed" upon already. Agreement about reality contributes to creating reality. Through his wife's death, Hightower learns important lessons about how the town will construct "facts" later, in Joe Christmas's case (and, by implication, in its overall handling of any undefined otherness): "that was all it required: that idea, that single idle word blown from mind to mind." Fictions seem inevitable, and their "ingenuity" recalls the constructs of Don Quixote, the ingenioso hidalgo. Hightower thinks that "ingenuity was apparently given man in order that he may supply himself in crises with shapes and sounds with which to guard himself from the truth": by now he knows this statement is apt, and most of all apt in his own case.

Joe's End: The "Coherence" Problem

Yet we must ask at the end to what extent Faulkner himself hides from a truth he has uncovered, mainly by encasing it in an overcomplex, even dual, narrative structure. Let us turn to the most frequently encountered critical crux of the novel, the "coherence" problem. The peculiar quality of *Light in August* derives from the manner in which it encloses an indeterminate character within a construct that struggles to give that character's life and death a significance. Faulkner, answering the criticism that his novels were merely short stories patched together, assured Ben Wasson after writing *Light in August* that "this one is a novel, not an anecdote," but less than a year later F. R. Leavis was to call the elements of the novel "unrelated organically." Another critic suggests that the "difficulty has always come with the attempt to relate the various episodes so as to show a coherent pattern of meaning. Critics so generally sympathetic as Conrad Aiken and George Marion O'Donnell find the novel a failure because of lack of unity." It should be clear by now, however, that such a project of creating an organic "unity" or "coherent pattern of meaning" would involve us in the very same procedure of misrecognition that society uses to force Christmas to be "one thing."

As in *The Wild Palms,* and to an extent *Go Down, Moses,* Faulkner would "freeze" the meaning of an indeterminate signifier. The very cyclicality of the enveloping Lena Grove story is striking. The symbolism of her circular road ("My, my. A body does get around," she repeats) is an apparently redemptive counterpoint to Joe's linear, fateful, and "tragic" road to death. The powers of darkness and bigotry would, according to this interpretation, be overturned by the forces of fertility, the "fundamental permanence of the earth" represented by Lena. The novel ends with the tale of how Lena sexually excites and then restrains Byron Bunch. The comic narration here is told by a furniture dealer to his wife in bed. The fact that the teller "shows" his wife what Bunch "wanted to do" with Lena—he makes love to her, rather than telling her "Bunch wanted to make love to Lena"—may represent a victory of deeds over words, activity over sterile talking. Even this final possibility, however, explicitly cancels out any sense that a verbally communicable lesson may be learned from the Christmas story.

Instead of the "tale later," the furniture dealer's wife gets "action sooner," yet the need to create meanings sooner or later is powerful enough that no one can claim to be escaped, not even Christmas himself. Joe Christmas learns that he has to be black, because "If I'm not, damned if I haven't wasted a lot of time." He lives among blacks, "trying to breathe into himself the dark odor, the dark and inscrutable thinking and being of negroes . . . trying to expel from himself the white blood and the white thinking and being." But even here the narrator has learned nothing. The narrator, unable to suspend judgment about Joe's true "being," says "white blood."

Despite the comic denouement, Christmas's tragic death provides the true climax of the novel. Interestingly syntax becomes suddenly ambiguous in this scene. The uncertainties surrounding the meaning of Joe Christmas's murder implicate author, town, and reader in the same web of guilt. We all owe a debt, of sorts, to any victim. Manifestly, in this case, his observers have crucified Christmas (or allowed him to be crucified), and his death has made a good yarn for the public:

> Then his face, body, all, seemed to collapse, to fall in upon itself, and from out the slashed garments about his hips and loins *the pent black blood* seemed to rush like a released breath. *It* seemed to rush out of his pale body like the rush of sparks from a rising rocket; upon that *black blast* the man seemed to rise soaring into their memories forever and forever. *They* are not to lose *it*, in whatever peaceful valleys, beside whatever placid and reassuring streams of old age, in the mirroring faces of whatever children *they* will contemplate old disasters and newer hopes. *It* will be there, musing,

> quiet, steadfast, not fading, and not particularly threatful,
> but of *itself* alone serene, of *itself* alone triumphant. (My
> italics)

This long excerpt may be the most important passage in the novel for
tracing Faulkner's ambiguous conclusions. At least two things are
striking in this tableau of Joe Christmas's martyrdom. In the first
place, the various fatal ambiguities concerning "white" and "black'
blood come to a head, without being at all resolved. What is "the pent
black blood?" Whether "black" is here a figurative or literal term is
crucial, but impossible to determine. Does this idea of "black blood"
share in Calvin Burden's idea of a curse of blackness "staining their
blood and flesh" or Gavin Stevens's elegant schematics of "white blood"
and "black blood"?

Moreover, the "blood" would seem to be the antecedent of "It"
in the next sentence. "It" is the "black blast" upon which the figure of
Christmas rises, apotheosized into an elegiac mode of memory. Faulkner has made the scene into a tableau, a "frozen moment," in which
we would preserve in "memory" what he deems important. This
"memory" is above all the written text, and the lesson, such as it is,
has been made at the expense of a life. Certainly, though, the image
that has been "fixed" here as permanent and self-sufficient ("not fading
. . . of itself alone triumphant") only leads to more instability—particularly
in the interpretation of "black blood." Who are the "They" of this
excerpt? Who actually remembers the death of Christmas? "They are
not to lose it. . . . It will be there, musing, quiet, steadfast." "They"
must certainly refer to the same people as in "their memories." But the
memory is as ambiguous as the "they" who remember. Either "It"
may be a condemnation of the inhumanity, or "It" may be a warning
to the "niggers" of Jefferson—as such murder/castrations tended to
be—about how *not* to behave with whites in general and white women
in particular. "Pantaloon in Black" gives a similarly striking example
of Southern "pedagogy" for blacks, an unwritten education by violence. After the black hero Rider kills a white man, we find "the
prisoner on the following day, hanging from the bell-rope in a negro
schoolhouse about two miles from the sawmill" (*Go Down, Moses*).
The blacks in Jefferson can be expected to remember every nuance of
the Christmas story, including the fact that Joe was probably white.
"The town," on the other hand, while remembering the tableau, will
probably repress how and why Christmas died, as Hightower does

above. This forgetting would be in accord with the general style of the town. As [Theodor] Adorno suggests, "all reification is a forgetting": Jefferson cannot remember the truth without losing its flattering and fixed self-image. For the town, Joe Christmas will always be "the nigger" who slit the "white woman's" throat and "got what he deserved."

In the end, the town, which seems "peaceful" and "placid" soon after the murder, does not choose between possibilities. The "memory" is only a potentially recapturable trace. Once we extend the possible referent of the "they" to Faulkner's readers, we can perhaps account for the confusion about the meaning of *Light in August*. With few exceptions, such investigations into "coherence" remain unsatisfying as descriptions of the "It" that Faulkner has promised will not even need justification ("of itself alone triumphant"). The ironic thing—which no doubt did not escape Faulkner—is that if we actually follow his narrator here, who offers a "serene" and "triumphant" recollection of a vigilante murder, then we have but murdered Joe Christmas once again.

Murder and the Communities: Ideology in and around *Light in August*

John N. Duvall

In a recent essay, André Bleikasten called for an ideological study of the texts of William Faulkner. "The conspicuous absence, in Faulkner criticism, of any substantial and serious consideration of the ideological aspects of his fiction," argues Bleikasten, indicates the desire of Faulkner studies to present Faulkner as a "moderate conservative or moderate liberal." Bleikasten points to Cleanth Brooks's well-known reading of *Light in August,* in which the pariah is set against the cohesive community, as an example of this conservatism: "Nowhere does [Brooks] allow for the possibility that the rejection of culturally standardized roles might spring from a sane impulse of self-preservation, and that, conversely, social conformity might be crippling." For Brooks,

> *Unless the controlling purposes of the individual are related to those that other men share and in which the individual can participate, he is isolated and is forced to fall back upon his personal values, with all the risks of fanaticism and distortion to which such isolation is liable.*
>
> *The community is at once the field of man's action and the norm by which his action is judged and regulated.*

Brooks's conservatism manifests itself in a number of other ways, none so vivid, perhaps, as his description of Hightower's beating. The text clearly identifies the KKK as the group responsible; Brooks calls the

From *Novel: A Forum on Fiction* 20, no. 2 (Winter 1987). © 1987 by Novel Corp.

attackers "some men," silently erasing a piece of Southern history he might prefer not to acknowledge. Brooks's work still influences the arguments of a new generation of Faulkner scholars. Even, for example, in a study as involved with radical theory as Donald Kartiganer's *The Fragile Thread* (with its references to Barthes, de Man, Derrida, and Nietzsche), Brooks's position on the community is reaffirmed: "We shall not reach the deepest meanings of *Light in August* . . . by attacking the community. It is, for the bulk of the novel, a quiet, peaceful place, precisely because it has worked out a modus vivendi of pattern and desire that enables it to endure and protect its members." Yet beneath this peace and quiet lurks sinister intention, as illustrated in the community's reaction to Byron Bunch's aiding Lena Grove. Brooks feels that from the outset Byron is another outsider and that only when he becomes involved with Lena is he "brought back into the community." Yet one could reasonably argue that Byron becomes a pariah only *after* he becomes involved with Lena. While it is true that his fellow workers consider him somewhat naive ("I reckon Byron stays out of meanness too much himself to keep up with other folks"), there is no hint of animosity towards him and the workers share their best stories and gossip with him. But after Byron begins helping a strange, pregnant woman, going so far as to put her in the cabin behind the ruins of the Burden house and living himself in a tent just a little way off, the rumor that Byron is the father begins to circulate. After Lena has her child and Brown/Burch is sent to marry Lena, both Mrs. Beard and the sheriff in turn ask Byron, kindly but with unmistakable undertones of the communal intolerance, about his future plans: "You're figuring on leaving right away, I reckon." It doesn't matter that Byron has not actually violated the community's sexual code; he has upset its moral sensibility, and he is asked very politely to leave. Hightower's narrative of course reminds us of what happens to one who does not take the polite hint.

In part, Thadious M. Davis answers Bleikasten's call. Davis's chapter on *Light in August* often reads like a sustained argument with Brooks, though she attributes his positions to "the reader":

> While the reader may assume the existence of a traditional community in Light in August *(largely oriented toward rural, agrarian, familial values), the reader perhaps should not automatically assume that its morality is an ideal norm. In the world of Jefferson as much fanaticism and misperception lie within the white community*

*as without. . . . Faulkner does not uncritically celebrate the com-
munity or uphold its standards of religion, race, sex, or ethics. In
fact, a major cause of ambiguity in Faulkner may well stem from
his own inability to determine exactly how to remain a part of a
flawed community while exposing its flaws and questioning the
validity of its fundamental assumptions.*

Davis argues that, despite differences in personality, education, and
class, most characters' thoughts on race are the product of white
supremacist ideology and that there are certain moments when the
reader may become implicated in the same ideology that the text
problematizes. Thus, white supremacy manifests itself whether it be
through the sheriff's "get-me-a-nigger" attitude, Doc Hines's fanatical
preaching, Gavin Stevens's theorizing, or Percy Grimm's patriotism.
We too may find ourselves surprised by ideology if we "applaud
[Joe's] final 'peaceful' return to Jefferson wearing 'nigger' shoes" since
that impulse "is a tacit admission that the survival of order and moral-
ity in southern life depends upon the existence of the 'nigger' " or if
we react like the men who "dread and expect the outcome" of Percy
Grimm's castration of Christmas. But despite Davis's exposure of the
interpretive community's complicity in the racist ideology of Jefferson,
she replicates another judgment which is a consensus in Faulkner
studies and which has ideological implications as entrapping as those
she has laid bare, simply by calling Joe Christmas a murderer.

I

*Well, Joe Christmas—I think that you really can't say that any man is good
or bad. I grant you there are some exceptions, but man is the victim of
himself, or his fellows, or his own nature, or his environment, but no man is
good or bad either. He tries to do the best he can within his rights. . . .
And I don't think he was bad, I think he was tragic.*

WILLIAM FAULKNER

Miss Joanna Burden's, where Christmas killed Miss Burden.
Faulkner's map of Yoknapatawpha, *Absalom, Absalom!*

*Because that was all it required: that idea, that single idle word blown from
mind to mind.*

Light in August

To begin reassessing the idea of community in *Light in August*, I would
like first to address how and what the interpretive community calls Joe

Christmas's killing of Joanna Burden. This may be regarded by some as trivial, but I have chosen this way into the text in the belief that what is casually taken for granted often betrays deep ideological investments. This belief is predicated on ideas of Freud, Lévi-Strauss, Althusser, and Bakhtin/Vološinov that question traditional notions of the author's control in the production of textual meanings. My argument with mainstream Faulkner criticism, which I hope to bring out by examining the killing, is twofold. First, accepting a traditional understanding of authorship negates the possibility of examining the political unconscious in Faulkner's texts, by considering them as a form of cultural myth. The traditional authoritarian conception of the production of textual meaning, as Foucault suggests, asserts ineffable genius—the author as a superior unified subject says what s/he means ("What Is an Author?"). In contrast, the psychosemiotic position views even the psyche of the author as a social construction; the speaker/writer necessarily means more than s/he intends. These two contrasting ways of explaining the production of meaning create, in a sense, a textual version of the debate on free will and determinism.

To posit genius ignores much of what has been thought about narrative and the unconscious in this century. Freud, for example, says of dream narratives: "A dream does not want to say anything to anyone. It is not a vehicle for communication; on the contrary, it is meant to remain ununderstood" (*Introductory Lectures on Psychoanalysis*); Lévi-Strauss claims to show not "how men think the myths, but rather how the myths think themselves out in men and without men's knowledge" ("Overture to *le Cru et le cuit*"). In short, dreams speak to us, in unrecognizably distorted form, of something about ourselves that we don't want to know; myths tell us in code, again distorted, something about our culture that we would prefer not to know. For both Freud and Lévi-Strauss, the way to read these encoded messages is to devalue contiguity, linearity, and cause and effect and to look instead for narrative's signification in the atemporal grouping of homologous units. My second dissatisfaction focuses on the lack of self-reflexivity in the discourse of Faulkner studies. Reflective thinking alone can interrupt the illusion of innocence in interpretive writing by forcing one to consider her or his relation to ideology. For Althusser, if I may bring together statements from "Marxism and Humanism" (*For Marx*) and "Ideology and Ideological State Apparatuses" (*Lenin and Philosophy*), ideology is a "profoundly *unconscious*" "system (with its own logic and rigour) of representations (images, myths, ideas or concepts)" "of the subject's real conditions of existence." The particular system of representation about which we, as writers writing about writing, should be most concerned is language. Bakhtin/Vološinov perceives language as an inescapable zone of ideological representation: "The logic of consciousness is the logic of ideological communication, of the semiotic interaction of a social group." Hence, "the word is the fundamental object of the study of ideologies" because of its constitutive role in consciousness and communication (*Marxism and the Philosophy of Language*). For Bakhtin/Vološinov, since language is a belief system, every word is ideological and hence the potential site of legitimate political struggle. (There is no zero degree of ideology, and I do not claim an unbiased position. This essay opposes the dominant and conservative paradigm in Faulkner studies—the cohesive community, with the family as its minimal unit, a unit which requires the rigid maintenance of gender roles. This paradigm is the inheritance of Faulkner studies from Southern Agrarianism, via Cleanth Brooks's rhetorically persuasive readings of Faulkner. For a more detailed discussion of the way Southern Agrarianism still speaks through the discourse of Faulkner studies, see my "Faulkner's Critics and Women." Later in this essay I refer to some of the implications that adhere to our calling Joe Christmas a murderer.) One particular word that gives us an entry into the ideological unconscious of the discourse of Faulkner studies on *Light in August* is *murder*—"the unlawful killing of a human being with malice aforethought" (*OED*). Although the sole owner and proprietor of Yoknapatawpha County chooses the less connotatively charged *kills* to describe the act, nearly every critic in the political spectrum from Cleanth Brooks to the Marxian, Myra Jehlen, agrees that Joe *murders* Joanna. I would like to suggest, however, that when we hail Joe Christmas as murderer, we hail ourselves in the moment of our own speaking as members of the textual community (Jefferson) and the extra-textual or interpretive community. Moreover, we involve ourselves in sexist (as well as racist) ideology when we call Joe a murderer.

I use the pronoun "we" in the above paragraph because I too in my teaching and thinking about *Light in August* have made the easy and immediate judgment that Christmas is a murderer. The text pushes one to such a conclusion in a number of ways. We are prepared both before and after the fact to choose "murder" as the word to describe Christmas's act. It is only fitting that Byron Bunch (whether one believes him to be of the community or not) should be the first to speak the word "murder" since he consistently absorbs and reflects the

words of the community in his function as intra-homo-diegetic narrator. Even before Brown/Burch betrays Christmas "to avoid being
accused of the murder itself," Byron reveals that Joanna's death is
immediately perceived as murder: "The sheriff found out how some-
body had been living in that cabin, and then right off everybody begun
to tell about Christmas and Brown, that had kept [their selling whiskey]
a secret long enough for one of them or maybe both of them to
murder that lady." Certainly chapter 5 seems to establish "malice
aforethought." Two moments are particularly damning: first, there is
Christmas's thought while standing over Brown/Burch, *"This is not
the right one,"* which establishes "the razor with its five inch blade" as a
lethal weapon; second, there is his statement seeming to provide a
motive: "She ought not to started praying over me. She would have
been all right if she hadn't started praying over me." Yet the repetition
of the sentence "Something is going to happen to me," with its
resonances within the Faulknerian universe, begins to work in another
direction; for Temple Drake in *Sanctuary,* the Reporter in *Pylon,* and
Harry Wilbourne in *The Wild Palms* their use of the same line suggests
their victimization rather than their agency. When chapter 12 picks up
where Chapter 5 leaves off with Joe preparing to mount the stairs to
confront Joanna, his thoughts still suggest an intent to kill Joanna: "he
believed with calm paradox that he was the volitionless servant of the
fatality in which he believed that he did not believe. He was saying to
himself *I had to do it* already in the past tense; *I had to do it. She said so
herself."* Even the intervening pages in chapters 6–12, generally seen as
humanizing the murderer, present us with incidents that prepare us for
Joe's "murder" of Joanna. For example, there is Joe's violence against
women in his attack on the black girl and later on the prostitute who
was unconcerned with his racial background; also we see Joe strike his
adoptive father with a chair. This makes Joe a double murderer for
some critics who forget that McEachern was attacking Joe (who has
been the victim of child abuse at the hands of his adoptive father) and
that McEachern may have survived the blow to the head.

The opening of chapter 13 follows just three pages after the
climactic moments leading up to . . . that crucial absence in both the text
and Joe's memory that withholds the details of Joanna's death and
presents a fuller version of the community's reaction to her death than
we get from Byron's second-hand information that he shares with
Hightower in chapter 4. We are manipulated again at the manifest level
into acceding to the community's judgment by the repetition of the

same "murder." *"Murdering a white woman the black son of a,"* says a disembodied voice in the crowd at the fire. There is the "thousand dollars' reward for the capture of [Joanna's] murderer" offered by her nephew. Additionally, Christmas's attack upon the congregation of a rural church, particularly his striking Roz Thompson (which for some critics means that Joe is a three-time murderer), makes it easier to hail Christmas as murderer in his killing of Joanna.

Even the "semi-omniscient" narrator seems to lend his voice to the chorus crying murder. There is a statement following the arrival of the bloodhounds: "It was as if the very initial outrage of the murder carried in its wake and made of all subsequent actions something monstrous and paradoxical and wrong, in themselves against both reason and nature." But if we use a more Genettian and Bakhtinian perspective to examine the discourse, then the extra-hetero-diegetic narrator speaks for the "men who had not slept very much since the night before last." In another instance, the narrator reports the speech of the country boy whom Christmas had flagged down with the pistol: "The boy told of having been on the way home in a car late Friday night, and of a man who stopped him a mile or two beyond the scene of the murder, with a pistol." Again we see a kind of indirect discourse in which the word "murder" is as much the boy's as it is the narrator's (and as much the community's as it is the boy's).

In the scene in which Christmas confronts Joanna on the night she is killed, what do we really know? Yes, Joe's thoughts have been bloody and violent; he thinks in fact of his killing of Joanna as already accomplished. Also we know that both lovers have agreed that "there's just one other thing to do." (We should not read Joanna's agreement that there is one other thing to do as a sign that she desires her own death in a kind of feminine masochism. Rather, this moment could be read as the arrangements for a duel, a structure in Faulkner we would have no trouble accepting if the two characters were male.) But when he enters her room on that fateful evening, Joanna asks him to light the lamp. He initially responds threateningly: "It won't need any light"; but then, leaving his unopened razor on the table, he complies with her request and lights the lamp. His defiance in refusing to pray, which recalls his childhood refusal to learn his catechism, is not violent but merely stubborn.

What is important here is to see what object Joanna as subject has in view at this moment. The passage leading up to the white space in which Joanna's death occurs is crucial:

> *Then he saw her arms unfold and her right hand come forth from beneath the shawl. It held an old style, single action, cap-and-ball revolver almost as long and heavier than a small rifle. But the shadow of it and of her arm and hand on the wall did not waver at all, the shadow of both monstrous, the cocked hammer monstrous, backhooked and viciously poised like the arched head of a snake; it did not waver at all. And her eyes did not waver at all. They were as still as the round black ring of the pistol muzzle. But there was no heat in them, no fury. They were calm and still as all pity and all despair and all conviction. But he was not watching them; he was watching the shadowed pistol on the wall; he was watching when the cocked shadow of the hammer flicked away.*

Although Joe is the cognitive subject ("he saw"), focalizing our perceptions in this passage, Joanna is the pragmatic subject and her object, which has been to get Joe to pray with her, is not to kill him, and but for the failure of the loaded gun to fire, she would have succeeded. This estrangement of the common-sense judgment about who acts in this moment is re-enforced by the realignment of the snake image. In chapter 2 Byron thinks of how Christmas's name ought to have been an "augur" like "a rattlesnake its rattle" and how he works like a man "chopping up a buried snake." In this instance it is Joanna who is associated with the snake ("the cocked hammer . . . poised like the arched head of a snake"). Is Christmas a murderer if he kills his attempted killer?

The vast majority of commentators never question Joe's guilt; it is, however, interesting to observe the tortuous ways in which critics who begin to sense some contradiction have described this fatal encounter that enable them still to label Joe's act a "murder." One critic, for example, suggests that the "final provocation is [Joanna's] *threatening* [Joe] with a pistol" and that she is "*apparently* prepared to kill Joe" (Pitavy, emphasis added). But surely pulling the trigger of a gun at point blank range is more than an apparent threat. An even stranger juxtaposition may be seen in observations of another critic who sees the potential for calling Christmas's act "self-defense," but then concludes that "the de facto explanation may be that Joe retaliated by committing *murder* in his own *defense*" (Fadiman, emphasis added). What is odd here, of course, is the pairing of self-defense and murder, appellations which are mutually exclusive. Just as when Christmas strikes McEachern, isn't he acting in what could be called self-defense, not murder? If Joe's intent seems violent and murderous, surely Joanna in her calm religious insanity is equally murderous, if not more so, since she makes the first deadly move.

It is of course a moot point, as there is no trial, whether Christmas's act of killing Joanna could be seen as justifiable homicide, but it is a point that nevertheless bears brief pursuit. A general principle for justifiable homicide in Mississippi law that could have provided a precedent in 1932 was established in 1879 in *Cannon* v. *Mississippi:* "That one has malice against another does not deny him the right to kill the other in self-defense." In fact, "the right of self-defense may arise though one is defending himself against danger which he himself has provoked, so as to make the homicide justifiable" (*Patterson* v. *Mississippi,* 1898). Most telling of all perhaps is the ruling in *Pulpus* v. *Mississippi,* 1903: "The fact that defendant provided himself with a deadly weapon and sought another with a design to kill him, and was the aggressor in the encounter in which he killed deceased, did not deprive him of the right of self-defense, *if the killing was not pursuant to the original purpose to kill*" (*Mississippi Digest,* sec. 5, nos. 101–13, emphasis added).

And this is precisely what I would argue if I were playing Gavin Stevens in a trial—that Joe's willingness to reopen communication with Joanna constitutes a suspension of his original intent to kill her. If Joe had simply walked into Joanna's room and slit her throat, the word "murder" would undoubtedly be correct. But his decision to light the lamp and his laying aside the unopened razor are, it seems, signs of a willingness, even at this late moment, to work towards a reconciliation. The dialogue fails, however, because Joanna is unwilling to speak as a human being and becomes instead another avatar of an avenging God: "I don't ask [that you pray]. It's not I who ask it." Because she will be the avenger she pulls out the pistol and with almost no hesitation tries to kill Joe. As readers we are quite willing to supply motives for Joe's "murdering" Joanna. We may conclude, for example, that Joanna has come to represent every tormentor in Joe's life: she is McEachern praying over him (and Joe refuses three times in this last meeting to kneel with her as he had refused three times to learn his catechism); she is Doc Hines in her religious fanaticism; she is Mrs. McEachern through the parallel food throwing scenes; she is Bobbie Allen, only now the surprise is menopause instead of menstruation; she is the dietitian because of her sexual desire, association with food, and perhaps even because when the gun fails to discharge, she seems to deny an expected punishment. All these parallels may be relevant and may have flashed through Joe's mind in the moment of the pistol hammer's falling, but that doesn't make his killing in self-defense a murder. (For the purposes of this essay, I reduce the possible ways of viewing a killing to murder or self-defense. In fact there exists a third category, manslaughter, which comes into play in the everyday workings of the criminal justice system. Manslaughter, an unlawful killing without malice aforethought, mediates the grey area between murder and self-defense. Perhaps it would be metaphorically correct to place Christmas's killing of Joanna in this category, since Joe himself always stands in a grey middle ground, whether between black and white or masculine and feminine.) Joe's tragedy that Faulkner speaks of may be that Christmas kills the only persons he loves, and in his running away he is only perceived as a "nigger murderer." What the text suggests is that this communal judgment is doubly twisted, since Joe, in addition to being non-black, is non-murderer. That the community passes judgment without a trial should immediately call into question its correctness, and we are perhaps more culpable for accepting this judgment since we are allowed to see and know so much more than the community.

In the community's eyes Joe is a murderer because Brown/Burch calls him a nigger, because Joe runs away, and, significantly, because Joanna is a white woman. Thadious Davis argues cogently that the town's construction of Joanna as Southern womanhood despoiled by the Negro illustrates the working of racist ideology. But in the interpretive community's acceptance of "murder" into its discourse, there is a corresponding sexist ideology, disturbing in its near invisibility, that replicates the Jeffersonians' "nice believing." When we call her death "murder," we tacitly affirm that woman is victim (and we unknowingly participate in the crowd's hope that she has been raped) and that the death of a woman, keeper of the finer values of society, mother-sister-daughter though spinster, is somehow special, more important than that of a man. We take, it seems, a perverse pleasure, disguised as moral outrage, in the violent death of a woman. To place Joanna on equal ground (as combatant or duelist) with Joe in their final meeting would give her an agency, a subjectivity that would take all the romance out of her death; to see woman as victim is to see woman as passive object. Women, this attitude asserts, are people to whom things happen, not who make things happen, and certainly they can't (or won't) kill anyone. Misogyny and the idealization of women are constituted in the same impulse; they are the two sides to a single sheet of paper.

II

As semiotic principles operated sub rosa in my assessment of the ideological impact of the word "murder" (e.g., identifying the subject/object relations in the scene leading up to Joanna's death), I would like to turn to chapter 1 to suggest uses of a more overt semiotic approach. An important aspect of thinking semiotically is that one sets aside the notion of protagonist or hero; one can temporarily and experimentally center *any* character, no matter how minor, as subject, if that character is engaged with a verb of doing, in order to see what patterns, if any, emerge. Often this manuever results in no significant insight or gain, but it remains a technique available to the analyst because *every character is the subject of his or her narrative program.* A particularly important actant in A. J. Greimas's scheme is the destinator (*Semiotics and Language*). The destinator is part of Greimas's reworking of Propp's classification of agents in Russian folktales and combines Propp's donor and dispatcher. To identify a destinator is to move toward an understanding of what motivates a character and why that character has particular goals or objects. Destinators may be individual characters, but a repetition of the destinator function within a narrative may point to a social or ideological force. In chapter 1, Lena Grove's narrative program dominates because it occupies the most text and because her object—to find Lucas Burch—is foregrounded. For Lena, as Greimasian subject, her destinator is both nature and culture, more precisely how culture interprets nature: she becomes pregnant (a fact of nature) and her brother calls her a whore (a cultural judgment which valuates nature). Lena's older brother, then, is her particular destinator (the king giving the knight his quest, as it were), but as the spokesperson of culture he is also an embodiment of the more ideological destinator—culture (especially patriarchal language) reading nature (especially female sexuality)—which recurs in a great number of the novel's other narrative programs. Questions of female "promiscuity" (sexuality outside marriage) are seen through judgments implicit in patriarchal language which aim to control that sexuality; thus, Milly, the dietitian, Mrs. Hightower, and Bobbie Allen fall under varying degrees of censure and have their actions motivated, in part, by this social destinator, whether its particular manifestation is, respectively, Doc Hines, Joe

Christmas, Hightower's congregation, or McEachern. A most revealing relationship between destinator and destinatee is that of the child Christmas and the dietitian because it illustrates her construction of her own destinator. It is only the dietitian's paranoia, which causes her to believe that Joe would "want to tell [of her sexual encounter] as an adult would," that allows a child to become the embodiment of patriarchal judgment; thus the dietitian's internalization of the judgment which condemns her sexuality is projected onto Joe. She believes Joe would take a male's pleasure in revealing the virgin to be a whore. The failed contract between the dietitian and Joe—Joe's refusal to take the dollar bribe—results largely from the two parties' inability to perceive the others' immediate object: the dietitian wishes to avoid punishment; Joe, to accept punishment. Although this scene is presented humorously, the sexual politics underlying it are not comic.

Understanding the dietitian's fear of having her sexuality revealed requires that we think about the possibilities of female-male unions and of the woman's subjectivity within those unions. Repeatedly, communal voices in Faulkner's texts tell us that virginity is the only position for young, unmarried females to occupy. Every woman initially occupies this position, but through time, subject positions shift:

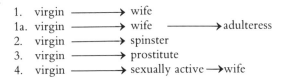

```
1.   virgin  ————→ wife
1a.  virgin  ————→ wife  ————→ adulteress
2.   virgin  ————→ spinster
3.   virgin  ————→ prostitute
4.   virgin  ————→ sexually active —→ wife
```

Just as virgin and wife are culturally privileged, only the movement from virgin to wife is positively marked as the ideal narrative. Yet a narrative movement recurring in Faulkner's fiction is the fourth one above, for which there is no middle term, per se; that is, there is no discreetly named subject position, and in male discourse this position is reduced to "whore," a term which inaccurately and moralistically names the action of this transitional stage. If a virgin takes or is taken by a premarital lover, she is called a whore, although she may later marry someone other than her premarital lover. This is the narrative, implied or represented, for Susan Reed in "Hair," Eula Varner Snopes in *The Hamlet*, Temple Drake in *Sanctuary* and *Requiem for a Nun*, Caddy in *The Sound and the Fury*, and Lena Grove in *Light in August*. We might chart the four primary subject positions as follows:

	sexually active	sexually inactive
positive	WIFE	VIRGIN
negative	PROSTITUTE	SPINSTER

Each of these four positions serves a social system, patriarchy, based on the perpetuation of the name of the father: a wife is a woman whose economic support derives from a sexual alliance with a man whose name and children she bears; a prostitute is a woman whose economic support derives from her alliances with men whose name and children she does not bear; a virgin is a presexual woman whose value as a commodity on the marriage market is high because of her strong potential for bearing a man's children and thus perpetuating his name; a spinster is a woman whose value on the marriage market has declined because of her doubtful ability to bear a man's children.

The problem now becomes reconciling these atemporal subject positions with the rules governing the sexual activity of women. I would suggest the following semiotic square as a way of understanding the female subject's position as a sexual being in the Faulknerian community:

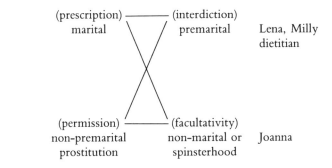

In the square above, the privileged position, from which difference generates, is occupied by the one overtly sanctioned zone of female sexuality—marriage; marriage alone is legally sanctioned because it gives males greater confidence in their paternity. Extramarital female sexuality, a position apparently missing in the above square, actually is contained within marital sexuality. Although certainly not sanctioned (since it undercuts the very function of giving males confidence in their paternity), extramarital female sexuality is not condemned as strongly by the community as premarital sexuality, providing the extramarital sexuality is discreet and thus honors the appearance of male dominance; the woman is still contractually and nominally the object of her husband. Power resides in the signifier (the father's name), not the signified; therefore, the patronymic and its perpetuation are a more overriding consideration in marriage than the genetic make-up of the offspring. Eula Varner Snope's affair with Manfred de Spain in *The Town,* for example, in no way undermines the patriarchal Flem Snopes, and in *Light in August* there are those who pity Mrs. Hightower because they believe the minister sexually deficient. Only when the extramarital sexuality becomes overt, as in *The Wild Palms,* does the community, textual and interpretive, condemn the woman.

Marriage's cultural binary, the contrary in this semiotic square, is premarital sexuality. Repeatedly father-figures condemn this type of female sexuality in the strongest language since it stands as the gravest threat to the name of the father; sexually active unmarried women, after all, bear children with no father-name. Premarital sexuality further threatens male power since it can potentially make a woman an acting agent inasmuch as the woman can enter the premarital relationship on more or less equal terms with the man; in all the other possible relations she is more object than subject. In *The Sound and the Fury* (Caddy and her daughter, Quentin) and *The Hamlet* (Eula) of course premarital sexuality figures prominently as part of the matter. Will Varner moves quickly in *The Hamlet* to erase Eula's "error" through a hasty marriage to Flem Snopes. In *Light in August,* Doc Hines brands both the dietitian and his daughter Milly as whores (as earlier Lena's brother had labeled her), which point to the contradictory of the contrary, non-premarital sexuality or prostitution. The lines of force, then, in this semiotic square suggest what labels adhere to the woman who sins by commission or omission and leads us to the subcontraries: to violate the premarital interdiction is to be a whore; to fail in the marital prescription is to be a spinster.

Significantly, male judgment is least harsh against the declared prostitutes since, although it disqualifies females from attaining marital status, it is less of a threat to (and, in fact may be seen as part of) the social fabric than either pre- or extramarital female sexuality in the Faulknerian world. In fact, prostitution forms a part of the social order since it contains a threat—unchecked female sexuality—within a limited internal space, the brothel, which usually men still control (even if a Miss Reba can take over for a Mr. Binford). Covertly sanctioned prostitution appears comically in *Sanctuary* through Miss Reba and her ladylike friends and tragically in *Absalom, Absalom!* and Charles Bon's

New Orleans. Prostitution is non-premarital since prostitutes form a set of women whom men almost never marry; therefore, prostitutes' sexuality does not pose a true threat to paternity. Even Lee Goodwin and Ruby (a former prostitute), who certainly form an alternative community in *Sanctuary,* are not married.

The fourth position represented on the semiotic square, non-marital, considers the limited sexuality of the "spinster." As a sexual being, if the wife has to have sex with a man (prescription), the virgin has not to have sex (interdiction), and the prostitute does not have not to have sex (permission), then the spinster does not have to have sex (facultativity). Spinsterhood, then, initially suggests a zone of independence from male authority, but this theoretical independence is as illusory as the prostitute's ghettoized "liberty." Social and economic pressures in the cohesive community make the spinster's apparent choice no choice at all. Two stories—"A Rose for Emily" and "Dry September"—particularly illustrate how the spinster's options are erased.

In addition to being the destinator of so many of the major and minor narrative programs of female characters in *Light in August,* culture attempting to enclose nature also drives Joe Christmas; he is a child of unknown parentage read as a "nigger bastard."

While Lena's narrative program dominates the novel's opening, other smaller but still meaningful narrative programs also play themselves out. For example, Armstid and Winterbottom both have narrative programs to the extent that they both have a particular economically motivated object in view, namely, their desire to profit in a deal concerning a piece of farm machinery. And while on the one hand the transaction between Armstid and Winterbottom represents a failed contract—Winterbottom rejects Armstid's offered price for the cultivator—in a semiotic sense, there has been a successful contract executed through their dialogue concerning Lena's origin. They represent, in effect, the community in miniature. Community always depends on the ability of at least two people to share a code or communication circuit, two people alternately appropriating that most free-floating of all signifiers, "I," in order to fix temporarily "you" and "s/he." The very nature of language necessitates an exclusion:

I/you ⟷ I/you	s/he
community	other

Jakobson's model of the communication circuit (of which the above is a modification) is crucial here insofar as we can think of it as a representation of a *minimal social unit* ("Linguistics and Poetics"). For Greimas, reciprocal communication constitutes a contract (again, semiotic if not always legal) (*Semiotics and Language*). By thinking of community in this fashion—two people sharing a communication circuit—we can begin to see that every conversation becomes an occasion during which the values of the hegemony are either confirmed or, in some way, called into question. Armstid and Winterbottom affirm their own identity as members of the larger community by identifying Lena as not of that community:

> *They saw at once that she was young, pregnant, and a stranger.* "I wonder *where she got that belly,*" Winterbottom said.
> "I wonder *how far she has brought it afoot,*" Armstid said.
> "*Visiting somebody back down the road,*" I reckon," Winterbottom said.
> "I reckon *not. Or I would have heard. And it ain't nobody up my way, neither. I would have heard that, too.*"
> "I reckon *she knows where she is going,*" Winterbottom said. "*She walks like it.*"
> "*She'll have company, before she goes much further,*" Armstid said. (Emphasis added)

In their desire to explain the presence of "a stranger," they demonstrate one of the functions of the community: curiosity ("I wonder") about a secret leads to posited causality ("I reckon"). This dialogue prefigures the planing mill workers' attempt to classify Christmas in chapter 2.

Besides sharing the common destinator of culture reading nature, Joe and Lena share a number of other structural parallels, many of which have been frequently noted, but which bear repeating here: both are orphans, who lead early lives of deprivation, expected to perform the work of adults as children; both respond to adolescent sexual longings and escape through windows to see their first lovers; both have their sexuality condemned by a father figure; their first lovers are both more sexually experienced and both lovers betray Joe and Lena, leaving them in trouble; both set off on the road in an attempt to resolve this trouble and, as noted above, both are immediately perceived as strangers, objects to be interpreted, when they reach Jefferson. Yet despite these similarities, it is their differences which are crucial: Lena is a female of certain parentage; Joe, a male of uncertain parentage. At the Armstids' Lena graciously accepts food; Christmas, however, who has not eaten for several days tells Byron, "I ain't hungry. Keep your muck." A reason Joe cannot accept food—while Lena can—is that to break bread obligates the recipient to share conversation, to engage in the social cont(r)act—an exchange of something good to think for something good to eat, as Lévi-Strauss might put it. To be able to narrate one's past, to share the story of one's origin with others is a key to community. Lena has little choice but to tell her story, since her condition is already an open sign, her quest for peace and happiness an external one—find and marry Lucas Burch; Joe, on the other hand, has literally nothing to tell, since his suspicion that he may have a part-black parent is one thing the white community will refuse to accept; thus his quest is internal—the peace and quiet of community he desires cannot be his as long as he cannot speak (of) himself. Byron notices that for Lena, "the telling never bothered her," while Christmas "did not talk to any of them at all." It seems at times as though the text were enumerating the structural possibilities of the stranger's relationship to speech: Lena, the stranger who speaks the truth about herself; Christmas, the stranger who speaks nothing about himself; Brown/Burch, the stranger who speaks lies about himself: Hightower, the estranged, who is prohibited from speaking about himself; and Joanna, the stranger who speaks only to the larger community's obverse reflection, the black community.

There are a number of moments in *Light in August* that remind us of the failure of language. For example, there is Calvin Burden who "read from the gilt and blazoned [Spanish Bible] in that language which none of them understood," which recalls Hightower's thoughts on Tennyson's language: "It is like listening in a cathedral to a eunuch chanting in a language which he does not even need to not understand." Joe Christmas, raised first in a white orphanage and then by white adoptive parents, fails in his attempt to merge with the black community because he finds blacks' "voices murmuring, talking, laughing, in a language not his." To the extent that language allows one to form alliances with others who share similar determinants, Joe's inability to participate in the language of the hegemony points us to a missing third term in the way the discourse of Faulkner studies speaks of the individual's relation to the community. Both Brooks's formulation of the problem and Bleikasten's and Davis's critiques of Brooks oppose the *individual* to the (hegemonic) *community*. But remembering the definition of the minimal constituent unit of community—two people sharing a code or circuit of communication—one realizes that an *alternative community* need only have two people in order to exist and by its very existence to imply a critique of the larger community.

Joe's first attempt at such an alliance is a failure. When he learns "with speech . . . about women's bodies" from Bobbie he attempts to narrate his origins: "He told her in turn what he knew to tell. He told about the negro girl in the mill shed. . . ." But when he tries truthfully to tell her "I got some nigger blood in me," her response is "You're what?" (not "you have what?" because for Joe to have "nigger blood" would mean he was a "nigger"). This is a subtle racist signifier of Bobbie's eventual betrayal; she reveals the "community" secret, as it were. It is metaphorically appropriate that Bobbie should be both a waitress and a prostitute, a female from whom one receives food and sex that is paid for, not shared, and though Joe temporarily is given a discount, he learns that one must eventually pay for one's pie. He does not understand his status as special customer, until he comes to take Bobbie away to marry her; he hasn't learned that a male does not marry his non-premarital lover.

Christmas and Joanna come much closer to achieving an alternative community. That they have a community is evident since they share food, social (communicative) and sexual intercourse. The community Joe and Joanna achieve is, to be sure, far from perfect—Joanna's racially motivated eroticism insures that this community, like the larger one it stands in opposition to, is flawed at base. But its greatest weakness, this eroticism, may be its greatest strength and certainly marks the relationship's counter-hegemonic force, since Joe finds a woman who not only accepts but is passionately attracted by the one piece of his history that he may not share with the hegemonic community—the possibility of a parent with mixed blood. Clearly Joe, who focalizes our perceptions of the relationship, finds the communion real and important. Another counter-hegemonic indicator is the relationship's inversion of the dominator/dominated binary. Joanna lives in the plantation house; Joe, in the slave's quarters. Thus the setting, which suggests female dominance, recalls that Joe, like Harry Wilbourne in *The Wild Palms,* finds his sexual partner to be a better man than he: "it was like I was the woman and she was the man."

The very detail in which Joe's relationship with Joanna is described signals its importance. Other than his relationship with Bobbie, his first love, his relations with other women, even the black woman with whom he "lived as man and wife," remain obscured; Joe's perceptions (and misconceptions) when he first sees Joanna create parallels to his first encounter with Bobbie and suggest that, once again, he has fallen in love at first sight. When Joe first sees Bobbie, she "did not look more than seventeen" to him, although "a casual adult glance" would reveal that she "would never see thirty again." Just as with Bobbie, he idealizes the female, and miscalculates Joanna's age: "By the light of the candle she did not look much more than thirty. . . ." And although the next day Joe, now capable of the "casual adult glance," realizes Joanna is much older, his construction of her is still locked into his initial image of "the woman at first sight of whom in the lifted candle (or perhaps the very sound of the slippered approaching feet) there had opened before him, instantaneous as a landscape in a lightningflash, a horizon of physical security and adultery if not pleasure." "Adultery if not pleasure" may not sound like love, but in light of his barely articulated goal, to enjoy the peace and comfort of community ("That's all I wanted"), this "physical security" coupled with sexuality is probably as close as he ever gets to this desire. Joe's relation with Joanna is not a static one, but rather one that, on Joe's part at least, grows into a deep and real love.

In the first phase of Joe and Joanna's relationship "[t]hey talked very little" or "with speech that told nothing at all since it didn't try to and didn't intend to." It is only when Joanna comes to narrate the story of her family—an act which signals the beginning of the second phase of the relationship—that the process of Joe and Joanna's shared language begins to gain a critical force. In fact, Joe interrupts Joanna's story to ask a most pertinent question for the whole of Light in August, a question that might well be asked of the Jeffersonian community: "Just when do men that have different blood in them stop hating one another?" Also in Joanna's narrative we see a recurrence of the patriarchal destinator. Without contradicting John T. Irwin's observation about the "motif of a grandchild whose destiny is determined by the life of the grandfather," I think we can still recognize the significance of Joanna's father. When Nathaniel takes Joanna, who is then four years old, to the cedar grove, he begins to pass on what he defines as the white man's curse. Later, in response to her dream of the crucified black infants, her father makes his role as destinator more explicit: "You must struggle, rise," he tells her, "But in order to rise, you must raise the shadow [the black race] with you. But you can never lift it to your level." In these two moments, Nathaniel Burden inscribes on Joanna the pattern of her desire.

After this meeting between Joe and Joanna, a social contract is established. Joe and Joanna begin to speak "in the fashion of lovers: that imperious and insatiable demand that the trivial details of both days be put into words, without any need to listen to the telling." A proof that this alternative community has a vitality can be seen in Joe's repeated decisions to leave which he never follows through with. Joe first decides to leave early in the relationship after he rapes Joanna, again toward the end of the second phase when she announces she is pregnant, and again the third phase when he finds the first note on his cot. It is in the third phase of the relationship when Joe and Joanna again become "strangers' that Joe realizes:

> When he first went to work, he would not need to think of
> [Joanna] during the day; he hardly ever thought about her. Now
> he could not help himself. She was in his mind so constantly that it
> was almost as if he were looking at her, there in the house, patient,
> waiting, inescapable, crazy.

When he receives her second note, the one he doesn't read, it is with relief, tenderness and a hope for renewed community:

> "All that damn foolishness. She is still she and I am still I. And
> now, after all this damn foolishness"; thinking how they would
> laugh over it tonight, later, afterward, when the time for quiet
> talking and quiet laughing came: at the whole thing, at one
> another, at themselves.

Although the alternative formation of Joe and Joanna violently expires because its two members break their circuit of communication in a return to their earlier self-reliant ways, we see another alternative community in the story of Lena Grove and Byron Bunch. For Byron to attain this alternative community, however, he must first renounce his affiliation with another private community, one he shares with Hightower.

In the weekly conversations of these two lonely men (a communion like Joe and Joanna's of which the larger community is ignorant), a kind of father/son relationship works itself out. For Gail Hightower, the relationship gives him more than just the son he never had. In a sense, this communion allows him to become his grandfather, the original Gail Hightower, and, in effect, to master the father who was "a stranger . . . a foreigner, almost a threat" by becoming the father of the father. Hightower's father, when he "just turned twenty-one, [rode] sixteen miles each Sunday to preach in a small Presbyterian chapel back in the hills." Similarly, Byron, as only Hightower knows, "rides thirty miles into the country and spends Sunday leading the choir in a country church." This connection helps us see how Hightower becomes, imaginatively, the "bluff direct" man his grandfather was. Although certainly a pale reproduction of the original, there is something of the grandfather in Hightower's customary manner of greeting Byron: "this faintly overbearing note of levity and warmth to put the other at his ease." Certainly Hightower attempts to appropriate the role of patriarchal destinator when he condemns Lena as an unsuitable marriage partner because she is not a virgin and clearly sets forth an object for Byron to accomplish: "Go Away. Now. At once. Turn your face now, and don't look back." Although the community of the two men is shattered at the moment Byron denies the will of the father figure, one should remember how very close Byron comes to following this directive.

Significantly, when Hightower lies to Percy Grimm in a vain attempt to save Christmas, the minister's actions are not entirely altruistic. Hightower apparently honors his surrogate son's request, one he earlier had furiously denied. In chapter 16 Byron asked Hightower to provide Christmas with an alibi—"You could say he was here with you that night. Every night when Brown said he watched him go up to the big house and go in it. Folks would believe you. They would believe that anyway"— so that Mrs. Hines could be reunited with her grandson. Byron counts on the townspeople's remembering the rumors concerning the minister and his black male cook; the townspeople, Byron suggests, would rather believe that Christmas is homosexual than that a black man had been sleeping with a white woman. Hightower initially reads Byron's request as part of the younger man's repudiation of their friendship or an affirmation of Byron's desire for Lena and so responds with bitterness:

> Ah. Yes. Yes. They would believe it. That would be very simple, very good. Good for all. Then [Christmas] will be restored to them who have suffered because of him, and Brown without the reward could be scared into making her child legitimate and then into fleeing again and forever this time. And then it would be just her and Byron. Since I am just an old man who has been fortunate enough to grow old without having to learn the despair of love.

When Hightower does make his appeal ("Listen to me. [Christmas] was here that night. He was with me the night of the murder"),

Byron's prediction about what people will remember comes true through Percy Grimm's words: "Jesus Christ. . . . Has every preacher and old maid in Jefferson taken their pants down to the yellowbellied son of a bitch?" In claiming to have been with Christmas "the night of the murder," Hightower interposes himself, however unfactually, as the active third party in a love triangle with Joe Christmas and Joanna Burden. This position solidifies Hightower's role as the mediator between Joe's and Lena's narratives since in both Joe and Joanna's and Byron and Lena's relationships, Hightower stands as the third party. The crucial difference is that in the false relationship (Joe–Hightower–Joanna), Hightower is a sexually acting being, while in the actual struggle (Byron–Hightower–Lena), the minister is ineffectual and can only watch as Byron's desire for Lena grows. It seems, then, that Hightower's hysterical refusal to go along with Byron's request becomes, in the minister's plea to Grimm, a displaced expression of his love for Byron: Christmas wasn't with Hightower, but Hightower wishes Byron had been.

Ultimately, Byron and Lena's relationship forms a more radical critique of the hegemonic community's patriarchal values than that of Joe and Joanna, which, once made public through Joanna's death, the community is able to read in a way that not merely denies the formation its counter-hegemonic force but also makes it the occasion to reaffirm the community's grossest stereotypes. Like Joe, Byron experiences love at first sight with his female "stranger." Byron accepts Lena's child, though, only after confronting what surely is the voice of hegemony, thinking itself through Byron: *"Byron Bunch, that weeded another man's laidby crop, without any halvers. The fellow that took care of another man's whore while the other fellow was busy making a thousand dollars. And got nothing for it."* This is Byron's construction, what he believes others are thinking of him; Byron's thoughts represent a kind of subjectification through the ideology that clings to language. Like the dietitian, Byron has internalized the patriarchal language of the hegemony, and he essentially hails himself as a fool.

In accepting Lena, however, Byron is much more than a fool; he is a traitor to the patriarchy. By taking a "whore" with a "bastard," Byron denies the normative judgment of Jefferson. What is perhaps more significant is that his loving Lena undercuts the foundation of the patriarchy—the name of the father; Byron accepts the role of husband and father while the biological father escapes. That Lena finds Byron occurs only through the similarity of Byron's name (Bunch) to that of the actual father (Burch), I am tempted to suggest, exemplifies the slippage of the signified (maternity) under the signifier (paternity); in this minimal difference of the signifier–r/n–Lucas may be seen as the self-castrating male (for what is the "r" but a castrated "n"?) who denies both patronymic and paternity. This gesture of trivializing paternity repeats itself even more explicitly in *Pylon* where the child's name, Jack Shumann, becomes a continually signifying absence; because the child is the product of an alternative community—the ménage à trois of Roger Shumann, Laverne, and Jack Holmes—his paternity has simply been lost.

If we take comedy as the individual's absorption into the community and tragedy as the individual's expulsion from the community, then, Joe and Joanna's tragic alternative community stands opposed to Lena and Byron's comic community. Certainly there are clear comic markers at the end of *Light in August:* rebirth, represented by Lena's infant, and marriage, at least implied in Byron and Lena's future (although in accepting the possibility of marriage, I may well be caught in a trap similar to speaking of Joe as a murderer). Yet the couple's expulsion from Jefferson works against this facile opposition. Brooks's jocular conclusion that "Byron needs to learn the mean between rape and Platonic love" merely repeats the (textual and interpretive) community's pattern of misogyny and idealization of women. Byron's attempted rape of Lena, which she certainly never perceives as a threat, recalls obliquely Joe's rape of Joanna. Byron's attempt lacks the violence of Joe's attack, yet Byron's desire to take Lena sexually, even though he goes about it "like he had eggs under his feet," expresses a wish to assert a masculine authority. Byron's failure to establish his authority, then, presents another moment when he overcomes the voice of patriarchy which tries to define his sexuality and behavior. If Byron, after ludicrously failing to subdue Lena, had acted as a conventional male, his relationship with her would have ended, since his humiliation at being physically weaker than the woman would not have permitted him to face her again. Like Joe, he returns to his loved one; Lena, unlike Joanna, is willing to accept the offer of renewed community. In accepting Byron's return, Lena assures that their alternative community will survive as a continuing commentary on the larger community.

Chronology

1897	Born William Cuthbert Falkner, in New Albany, Mississippi, on September 25; first child of Murry Falkner, then a railroad executive, and Maud Butler.
1914	Leaves school after long history as a poor student.
1916–17	Lives on fringe of student community at the University of Mississippi.
1918	Tries to enlist in U.S. armed forces, but is refused. Works in New Haven, Connecticut, for Winchester Gun factory. Changes spelling of name from "Falkner" to "Faulkner." Enlists in Canadian Air Force, but war ends while he is still in training.
1919	Returns to Oxford and enters the University of Mississippi. Writes poems that will be included in *The Marble Faun*.
1920	Leaves the university, but remains in Oxford.
1921	After spending autumn in New York City, returns to Oxford to work as postmaster.
1924	Resigns postmastership; *The Marble Faun*.
1925–26	New Orleans period, frequently in circle surrounding Sherwood Anderson. Writes *Soldiers' Pay* and *Mosquitoes;* travels to Europe and resides in Paris; returns to Oxford.
1927	Writes *Flags in the Dust,* which is rejected.
1928	Writes *The Sound and the Fury*.
1929	*Sartoris* (curtailed version of *Flags in the Dust*) published. Marriage of Faulkner and Estelle Franklin on June 20. Finishes *Sanctuary;* publishes *The Sound and the Fury;* begins *As I Lay Dying*.
1930	Finishes and publishes *As I Lay Dying;* revises *Sanctuary*.
1931	Daughter Alabama is born in January and dies the same month. *Sanctuary* published; begins *Light in August*.

1932	Finishes *Light in August,* which is published after his father's death; begins first Hollywood screenwriting period.
1933	*A Green Bough;* daughter Jill born.
1934	*Doctor Martino and Other Stories.*
1935	*Pylon.*
1936	*Absalom, Absalom!*
1938	*The Unvanquished.*
1939	*The Wild Palms.*
1940	*The Hamlet.*
1942	*Go Down, Moses.*
1946	*The Portable Faulkner,* edited by Malcolm Cowley.
1948	*Intruder in the Dust.*
1949	*Knight's Gambit.*
1950	*Collected Stories;* Nobel Prize in literature.
1951	*Requiem for a Nun.*
1954	*A Fable.* First assignment for State Department, as goodwill ambassador.
1955	Travels to Japan for State Department; Pulitzer Prize for *A Fable.*
1957	*The Town.*
1959	*The Mansion.*
1960	Faulkner's mother dies.
1962	*The Reivers.* Faulkner dies in Byhalia, Mississippi, on July 6, from coronary occlusion.

Contributors

HAROLD BLOOM, Sterling Professor of the Humanities at Yale University, is the author of *The Anxiety of Influence, Poetry and Repression,* and many other volumes of literary criticism. His forthcoming study, *Freud: Transference and Authority,* attempts a full-scale reading of all of Freud's major writings. A MacArthur Prize Fellow, he is general editor of five series of literary criticism published by Chelsea House. During 1987–88, he served as Charles Eliot Norton Professor of Poetry at Harvard University.

DONALD M. KARTIGANER teaches at the University of Washington. He is the author of *The Fragile Thread: The Meaning of Form in Faulkner's Novels.*

ANDRÉ BLEIKASTEN, a preeminent Faulknerian in France, teaches at the Universite de Strasbourg. His two books on Faulkner are *The Most Splendid Failure: Faulkner's* The Sound and the Fury and *Faulkner's* As I Lay Dying.

CAROLYN PORTER is Associate Professor at the University of California at Berkeley and the author of *Seeing and Being: The Plight of the Participant Observer in Emerson, James, Adams, and Faulkner.*

ERIC J. SUNDQUIST is Professor at the University of California, Berkeley. He has written *Home as Found: Authority and Genealogy in Nineteenth-Century American Literature* and has edited *American Realism: New Essays.* His most recent book is *Faulkner: The House Divided.*

JAMES A. SNEAD is Associate Professor of English and Comparative Literature at Yale University and the author of *Figures of Division: William Faulkner's Major Novels.*

JOHN N. DUVALL teaches at Iowa State University and is currently working on a book about marginal couples in Faulkner's novels of the 1930s.

Bibliography

Abadie, Ann J., and Doreen Fowler, eds. *Faulkner and the Southern Renaissance: Faulkner and Yoknapatawpha.* Jackson: University Press of Mississippi, 1982.

Adamowski, T. H. "Joe Christmas: The Tyranny of Childhood." *Novel: A Forum on Fiction* 4 (1971): 240–51.

Bassett, John. *William Faulkner: An Annotated Checklist of Criticism.* New York: David Lewis, 1972.

———, ed. *William Faulkner: The Critical Heritage.* Boston: Routledge & Kegan Paul, 1975.

Beck, Warren. *Faulkner: Essays by Warren Beck.* Madison: University of Wisconsin Press, 1976.

Bender, Eileen T. "Faulkner as Surrealist: The Persistence of Memory in *Light in August.*" *The Southern Literary Journal* 18, no. 1 (1985): 3–12.

Bidney, Martin. "Faulkner's Variations on Romantic Themes: Blake, Wordsworth, Byron and Shelley in *Light in August.*" *Mississippi Quarterly: The Journal of Southern Culture* 38 (1985): 277–86.

Bleikasten, André. "For/Against an Idealogical Reading of Faulkner's Novels." In *Faulkner and Idealism: Perspectives from Paris,* edited by Michel Gresset and Patrick S. Samway, Jackson: University Press of Mississippi, 1983.

Bloom, Harold, ed. *Modern Critical Views: William Faulkner.* New York: Chelsea House, 1986.

Blotner, Joseph L. *Faulkner: A Biography.* New York: Random House, 1974.

———. *Selected Letters of William Faulkner.* New York: Random House, 1977.

Brodhead, Richard H. *Faulkner: New Perspectives.* Englewood Cliffs, N.J.: Prentice-Hall, 1983.

Brooks, Cleanth. *William Faulkner: The Yoknapatawpha Country.* New Haven: Yale University Press, 1963.

———. *William Faulkner: Toward Yoknapatawpha and Beyond.* New Haven: Yale University Press, 1978.

———. *William Faulkner: First Encounters.* New Haven: Yale University Press, 1983.

Burroughs, Franklin G., Jr. "God the Father and Motherless Children: *Light in August.*" *Twentieth Century Literature* 19 (1973): 189–202.

Chase, Richard. "The Stone and the Crucifixion: Faulkner's *Light in August.*" *The Kenyon Review* 10 (1948): 539–51.

Collins, R. G. "*Light in August*: Faulkner's Stained Glass Triptych." *Mosaic* 7, no. 1 (1973): 95–157.

Cowley, Malcolm. *The Faulkner-Cowley File: Letters and Memories, 1944–1962.* New York: Viking, 1966.

Davis, Thadious M. *Faulkner's "Negro": Art and the Southern Context.* Baton Rouge: Louisiana State University Press, 1983.

Duvall, John N. "Faulkner's Critics and Women: The Voice of the Community." In *Faulkner and Women: Faulkner and Yoknapatawpha*, edited by Doreen Fowler and Ann J. Abadie. Jackson: University Press of Mississippi, 1986.

Fadiman, Regina K. *Faulkner's* Light in August: *A Description and Interpretation of Its Revisions.* Charlottesville: University Press of Virginia, 1975.

Faulkner Studies, 1980–.

Feldman, Robert L. "In Defense of Reverend Hightower: It Is Never Too Late." *College Language Association Journal* 29, 3 (1986): 352–67.

Fowler, Doreen. "Faulkner's *Light in August*: A Novel in Black and White." *Arizona Quarterly* 40 (1984): 305–24.

———. "Joe Christmas and 'Womanshenegro.' " In *Faulkner and Women: Faulkner and Yoknapatawpha*, edited by Doreen Fowler and Ann J. Abadie. Jackson: University Press of Mississippi, 1986.

Godden, Richard. "Call Me Nigger!: Race and Speech in Faulkner's *Light in August. Journal of American Studies* 14, no. 2 (1980): 235–48.

Gray, Richard. *The Literature of Memory.* Baltimore: The Johns Hopkins University Press, 1977.

Guerard, Albert J. *The Triumph of the Novel: Dickens, Dostoevsky, Faulkner.* New York: Oxford University Press, 1976.

Gwynn, Frederick L., and Joseph L. Blotner, eds. *Faulkner in the University: Class Conferences at the University of Virginia, 1957–58.* New York: Vintage-Random, 1965.

Haselswerdt, Marjorie B. "Keep Your Muck: A Horneyan Analysis of Joe Christmas and *Light in August.*" In *Third Force Psychology and the Study of Literature*, edited by J. Bernard. Rutherford, N.J.: Fairleigh Dickinson University Press, 1986.

Hill, Jane Bowers. *Beyond Myth: Sexual Identity in* Light in August *and Other Novels by William Faulkner. Dissertation Abstracts International,* Ann Arbor, Michigan. 1986 May; 46(II): 3351A.

Hlavsa, Virginia V. "The Mirror, the Lamp, and the Bed: Faulkner and the Modernists." *American Literature* 57 (1985): 22–43.

Hoffman, Frederick J., and Olga W. Vickery, eds. *William Faulkner: Three Decades of Criticism.* New York: Harcourt, Brace & World, 1963.

Howe, Irving. *William Faulkner: A Critical Study.* 2d ed., rev. Chicago: University of Chicago Press, 1975.

Hungerford, Harold. "Past and Present in *Light in August.*" *American Literature* 55 (May 1983): 183–98.

Inge, M. Thomas, ed. *The Merrill Studies in* Light in August. Columbus, Ohio: Merrill, 1971.

Irwin, John T. *Doubling and Incest/Repetition and Revenge.* Baltimore: The Johns Hopkins University Press, 1975.

Jehlen, Myra. *Class and Character in Faulkner's South*. New York: Columbia University Press, 1975.

Jenkins, Lee. *Faulkner and Black-White Relations: A Psychoanalytic Approach*. New York: Columbia University Press, 1981.

Kartiganer, Donald M. *The Fragile Thread: The Meaning of Form in Faulkner's Novels*. Amherst: University of Massachusetts Press, 1979.

Kazin, Alfred. "The Stillness of *Light in August*." In *William Faulkner: Three Decades of Criticism*, edited by Frederick J. Hoffman and Olga W. Vickery. New York: Harcourt, Brace & World, 1963.

Kerr, Elizabeth. *William Faulkner's Gothic Domain*. Port Washington, N.Y.: Kennikat, 1979.

Korenman, Joan S. "Faulkner's Grecian Urn." *The Southern Literary Journal* 7 (Fall 1974): 3–23.

Krieger, Murray. *The Classic Vision: The Retreat from Extremity in Modern Literature*. Baltimore: The Johns Hopkins University Press, 1971.

McHaney, Thomas L. *William Faulkner: A Reference Guide*. Boston: G. K. Hall, 1976.

Matthews, John T. *The Play of Faulkner's Language*. Ithaca: Cornell University Press, 1982.

Meats, Stephen E. "Who Killed Joanna Burden?" *Mississippi Quarterly: The Journal of Southern Culture* 24 (1971): 271–77.

Meriwether, James B., and Michael Millgate, eds. *Lion in the Garden: Interviews with William Faulkner, 1926–1962*. Lincoln: University of Nebraska Press, 1980.

Millgate, Michael. *The Achievement of William Faulkner*. New York: Random House, 1966.

———, ed. *The American Novel: New Essays on Faulkner's* Light in August. New York: Cambridge University Press, 1987.

Minnesota Review 17 (1981). Special Faulkner issue.

Minter, David. *William Faulkner: The Writing of a Life*. Baltimore: The Johns Hopkins University Press, 1980.

Mortimer, Gail L. *Faulkner's Rhetoric of Loss*. Austin: University of Texas Press, 1983.

Nash, H. C. "Faulkner's 'Furniture Repairer and Dealer': Knitting Up *Light in August*." *Modern Fiction Studies* 16 (1970–71): 529–31.

Parker, Robert Dale. *Faulkner and the Novelistic Imagination*. Urbana: University of Illinois Press, 1985.

Peternel, Joan. "The Double in *Light in August*: Narcissus or Janus?" *Notes on Mississippi Writers* 15, no. 1 (1983): 19–37.

Pitavy, François L. *Faulkner's* Light in August. Translated by Gillian E. Cook. Bloomington: Indiana University Press, 1973.

———, ed. *William Faulkner's* Light in August: *A Critical Casebook*. New York: Garland, 1982.

Porter, Carolyn. *Seeing and Being: The Plight of the Participant Observer in Emerson, James, Adams, and Faulkner*. Middletown: Wesleyan University Press, 1981.

Reed, Joseph W., Jr. *Faulkner's Narrative*. New Haven: Yale University Press, 1973.

Sensibar, Judith L. *The Origins of Faulkner's Art*. Austin: University of Texas Press, 1984.

Slatoff, Walter J. *Quest for Failure: A Study of William Faulkner*. Ithaca: Cornell University Press, 1960.

Shaw, Patrick W. "Joe Christmas and the Burden of Despair." *Texas Review* 1, no. 2 (1980): 89–97.

Snead, James A. *Figures of Division: William Faulkner's Major Novels*. New York: Methuen, 1986.

Spenko, James Lee. "The Death of Joe Christmas and the Power of Words." *Twentieth Century Literature* 28 (Fall 1982): 252–68.

Stonum, Gary Lee. *Faulkner's Career: An Internal Literary History*. Ithaca: Cornell University Press, 1975.

Sundquist, Eric J. *Faulkner: The House Divided*. Baltimore: The Johns Hopkins University Press, 1983.

Taylor, Carole Anne. "*Light in August*. The Epistemology of Tragic Paradox." *Texas Studies in Literature and Language* 22 (1980): 48–68.

Taylor, Walter. "Faulkner's Nineteenth Century Notions of Racial Mixture and the Twentieth Century Imagination." *The South Carolina Review* 10 (1977): 57–68.

Vickery, Olga. *The Novels of William Faulkner: A Critical Interpretation*. Rev. ed. Baton Rouge: Louisiana State University Press, 1964.

Vickery, John B., and Olga Vickery. Light in August *and the Critical Spectrum*. Belmont, Cal.: Wadsworth, 1971.

Volpe, Edmond. *A Reader's Guide to William Faulkner*. New York: Farrar, Straus & Giroux, The Noonday Press, 1964.

Wadlington, Warwick. *Reading Faulknerian Tragedy*. Ithaca: Cornell University Press, 1987.

Wagner, Linda Welshimer, ed. *Four Decades of Faulkner Criticism*. East Lansing: Michigan State University Press, 1973.

Warren, Robert Penn, ed. *Faulkner: A Collection of Critical Essays*. Englewood Cliffs, N.J.: Prentice-Hall, 1966.

Williams, David L. *Faulkner's Women: The Myth and the Muse*. Montreal: McGill-Queens University Press, 1977.

Wittenberg, Judith Bryant. *Faulkner: The Transfiguration of Biography*. Lincoln: University of Nebraska Press, 1979.

———. "William Faulkner: A Feminist Consideration." In *American Novelists Revisited: Essays in Feminist Criticism*, edited by Fritz Fleischman. Boston: G. K. Hall, 1982.

Wyatt, David. "Faulkner and the Burdens of the Past." In *Prodigal Sons: A Study in Authorship and Authority*. Baltimore: The Johns Hopkins University Press, 1980.

Acknowledgments

"The Meaning of Form in *Light in August*" (originally entitled "*Light in August*") by Donald M. Kartiganer from *The Fragile Thread: The Meaning of Form in Faulkner's Novels* by Donald M. Kartiganer, © 1979 by the University of Massachusetts Press. Reprinted by permission of the University of Massachusetts Press, Amherst, Massachusetts.

"Fathers in Faulkner and *Light in August*" (originally entitled "Fathers in Faulkner") by André Bleikasten from *The Fictional Father: Lacanian Readings of the Text,* edited by Robert Con Davis, © 1981 by the University of Massachusetts Press. Reprinted by permission of the University of Massachusetts Press, Amherst, Massachusetts.

"The Reified Reader: *Light in August*" (originally entitled "The Reified Reader") by Carolyn Porter from *Seeing and Being: The Plight of the Participant Observer in Emerson, James, Adams, and Faulkner* by Carolyn Porter, © 1981 by Carolyn Porter. Reprinted by permission of Wesleyan University Press.

"The Strange Career of Joe Christmas" by Eric J. Sundquist from *Faulkner: The House Divided* by Eric J. Sundquist, © 1983 by the Johns Hopkins University Press, Baltimore/London. Reprinted by permission of the Johns Hopkins University Press.

"Figures of Division: *Light in August*" (originally entitled "*Light in August* [1932]") by James A. Snead from *Figures of Division: William Faulkner's Major Novels* by James A. Snead, © 1986 by James A. Snead. Reprinted by permission of the author and Methuen & Co.

"Murder and the Communities: Ideology in and around *Light in August*" by John N. Duvall from *Novel: A Forum on Fiction* 20, no. 2 (Winter 1987), © 1987 by Novel Corp. Reprinted by permission.

Index